THE LITTLE GIDDING PRAYER BOOK

THE
LITTLE GIDDING
PRAYER BOOK

SPCK

First published in Great Britain 1986
SPCK
Holy Trinity Church
Marylebone Road
London NW1 4DU

British Library Cataloguing in Publication Data

The Little Gidding prayer book.
  1. Prayer-books
  I. Title
  254′.13   BV250

  ISBN 0-281-04243-8

Typeset by CCC, printed and bound in Great Britain
by William Clowes Limited,
Beccles and London

CONTENTS

INTRODUCTION

During this century the Church throughout the world has seen a remarkable renewal of community life. In the New Testament the word for 'church' derives from the Greek *ecclesia*, used for an 'assembly', a 'coming together'; and the various metaphors used to describe the Church – such as a body with many parts, or a temple built of many stones – all point to close spiritual fellowship. In our own time, as society has become progressively less communal and individuals more isolated, so Christians have realized ever more clearly that the life and witness of the Church depend on her members drawing together in close bonds of friendship and love.

This service book has evolved over ten years, as a community of families and single people has sought to find a common pattern of life and worship. The members of the community are very diverse in their situations and backgrounds. There are young single people, married couples with children, and middle-aged and elderly members; some live in an isolated cluster of houses sharing common facilities, while others are scattered in ordinary villages and towns; some are in paid employment, while others work full time for the community; and the community is ecumenical with Anglican, Roman Catholic and Free Church members. This book contains both the daily worship of this motley band of people, and also its simple rule of life.

We offer it now to the wider Church in the hope that others may find it helpful. Individuals, families or small groups wanting a simple discipline of daily worship could readily adapt our service to their own needs. House groups wishing to include a simple communion service at their meetings may find the service contained here suitable; indeed we have used it in precisely this way at parish Lent groups. Others may wish actually to join this community, the Community of Christ the Sower, sharing fully in its corporate prayer and fellowship; and the community is open to members in any situation, from any Christian tradition.

FORMING THE COMMUNITY

Historically our inspiration comes from two remarkable Christian men of the early seventeenth century, Nicholas Ferrar and George Herbert. In 1626 Nicholas Ferrar, a young and successful merchant and politician, established a Christian community at Little Gidding, which was a deserted hamlet in the Huntingdonshire Wolds. The community was based on his own extended family, with his mother, and his elder brother and sister with their respective families, forming the core. They restored the old manor house and church, and established a simple pattern of daily worship, work and fellowship. George Herbert, one of the greatest Christian poets and hymn-writers in the English language, was a contemporary and close friend of Nicholas Ferrar, supporting and advising him in his experiment in community life. Having himself also been an ambitious politician, Herbert became prebend of Leighton Bromswold, a parish five miles south of Little Gidding; and he in turn sought to establish a similar pattern of corporate life and worship within his own vicarage and parish church.

Ferrar and Herbert shared the conviction that a life of regular corporate prayer and close spiritual fellowship is the calling not just of monks, nuns and priests – religious specialists – but of all Christian people, whatever their station and in whatever circumstances they live. In this they were responding to a vision which is central to the English Reformation. Their pattern of daily worship was the Morning and Evening Prayer of the Book of Common Prayer, in which Cranmer and his fellow-compilers had condensed and reworked the old monastic offices to become the daily worship for the whole church. Nicholas Ferrar in his large family household, and George Herbert in his rural parish sought to put this vision into practice. And it is this same vision which has brought into being the Community of Christ the Sower.

In 1977 a charitable trust bought the old farmhouse at Little Gidding, next to the chapel used by the Ferrars, and began to build houses round the old farm courtyard. Now a group of about twenty-five people lives there, running a small farm and various workshops and research projects. Other members of the community live both in villages nearby and scattered across the country. In 1986 the old manor house at Leighton Bromswold, standing next to the church, became a community guest house. It was originally built by the Duchess of

Lennox, George Herbert's patron and supporter, and she frequently welcomed guests who wished to visit the Ferrars.

The basis of our common life is a short service of daily prayer and a simple weekly communion service. At Little Gidding and Leighton Bromswold as many members as possible come together each morning for prayer. But there, as elsewhere, there are members with jobs or young children which prevent their attending corporate daily prayer; so the service is designed to be equally suitable for couples or individuals to use on their own. The communion service is usually held on Saturday evening – and sometimes in mid-week – so that members can attend their parish churches on Sunday; and here too the service is designed to be equally suitable for quite a large group – up to forty regularly attend at Little Gidding – or a small house group, or even a single family. In addition we meet together in groups each week to share a meal – an *'agape'* to use the ancient word. There are also four special annual services for which the whole community tries to come together, marking different aspects of our common life.

DEVELOPING OUR WORSHIP

Ferrar and Herbert are usually identified with the 'high church' tradition of Anglicanism; and to a great extent this is justified. Both placed great importance on the sacraments, and on the beauty of worship; and both had an open-mindedness and a love of the arts which their Puritan contemporaries disparaged. But equally they were firmly Protestant not only in doctrine but also in the fervent devotion of their worship, and in their love of the Scriptures; and Ferrar preferred that communion be celebrated in the Protestant manner, with the people gathered in fellowship around the Lord's table. Thus in the context of their time they were ecumenical.

In the present time the same spirit demands a different practice. From the outset it was clear that we should not use the Anglican forms of worship, not only because that would seem to deny the traditions of other churches, but more importantly because their wordiness and complexity – and sheer length – make them indigestible for most Christians today as their staple daily prayer. But a more fundamental problem also faced us: that the rules of at least some denominations prevent intercommunion, and yet a Christian community that does not share the bread and wine seems a travesty. Some felt we had no choice but, within the limited context of the community, to break those rules. At first we experimented with various modern rites, and from that experience began to develop our own forms, suited to the diverse situations and backgrounds of our members.

Two principles have guided the composition of these services. The first is to base the words of the services on the Bible, which is the common root of every Christian tradition. The verses and responses in the services are taken from the New Testament, and the psalms and collects are drawn from the rich poetry found throughout the Scriptures. The second principle has been to try to combine the order and the love of sacraments of the Catholic tradition, with the freedom and simplicity of the Evangelical. This too is scriptural in inspiration: from the accounts in the Book of Acts and in the Epistles, the worship of the early Church seems to have been warm and spontaneous, yet orderly and sacramental, including not only regular communion, but also laying on of hands as a sign of healing and of commissioning for ministry. In our own pattern of worship we simply try to imitate this example.

In our evolution as a community perhaps the hardest challenge has been – and continues to be – to distinguish those things which are essential to our corporate life as Christians from those which are not. There is in any group a centrifugal force, made all the stronger by the individualistic spirit of the times: any rule or common discipline can be seen as stifling the freedom of individuals, so that quite easily all corporate life can be lost. This is a problem with which parish churches – especially in the Church of England – are all too familiar. At the same time, however, there is a centripetal force: we are tempted to seek a false security through being bound by strict, all-embracing rules, and to desire a highly communal and enclosed way of life as a bulwark against the world.

We have sought to develop a simple and brief rule of life, which seems to contain the essence of Christian community – whether it is lived in a close-knit group such as at Little Gidding, or in a more dispersed group within a parish. The rule is to be found in the short introduction to each of the six services in the book; and the spirit of the rule is expressed in prayer and worship in the services themselves. Thus our rule of life and our worship are explicitly bound together.

USING THE SERVICES

The first service in the book is Daily Prayer. And to accompany this service there are at the back of the book the opening sentences, readings and collects, and a cycle of seventy-two psalms. In a group the psalms can be said antiphonally, with the leader saying the odd-numbered verses and the rest the even-numbered verses. Our experience is that if possible people should take it in turn to lead, and the leader should guide the open prayer, preparing two or three particular intercessions which in turn may stimulate others; this helps to prevent the prayer from becoming stale and routine. Within the Community of Christ the Sower a six-monthly intercession list is circulated to all members, so that a particular member is prayed for each day. When using the service alone it is tempting to read the psalms and Bible passages in silence – indeed if one is on a bus or a train going to work there may be little choice! But the danger is that one rushes through the service, not concentrating on the words, so that for most people it is more satisfactory to read the psalms and Bible passages out loud. If there is about two minutes' silence after the Bible readings and perhaps five minutes of free prayer, the service should last no more than about twenty minutes – which for even the busiest person is quite realistic.

The Communion service works best where people gather round the Lord's table. It is thus particularly suited for celebration in people's homes, where perhaps a coffee table can be used for the bread and wine, and the congregation can sit in easy chairs or on the floor. In church one can go back to the original practice of the Church of England, favoured by Nicholas Ferrar, where the table is placed in the middle of the chancel; at the time of the celebration the people come up and stand round the table, with the president on the north side. In the Community of Christ the Sower people of all denominations, as well as baptized children, receive the bread and wine; and anyone, authorized by the community's pastors, may preside. It must obviously be a matter of discretion and prayerful thought as to whether this is right in other contexts, or whether the conventions of a particular denomination should be followed. The service is composed so that the key parts of the celebration itself – the thanksgiving, the memorial, and the invocation of the Holy Spirit – are said by the whole congregation, to emphasize the shared priesthood of all the faithful.

The four other services are generally used only once a year. The Covenant service comes at the beginning of our liturgical year in early autumn, when we renew our commitment as members of the community and when newcomers join. The Stewardship service takes place usually soon after Christmas, near Epiphany: just as the wise men brought gifts to the child Jesus, we each put round the Lord's Table an object symbolizing some work we are able to do for others – an act of worship which can be comic as well as serious. During the weeks beforehand members have reviewed in depth their use of time and resources, and so the service marks the central importance of stewardship in Christian life. The service of Reconciliation, which we have during Lent, uses the sign of laying on of hands to symbolize the healing power of God, both in bringing wholeness of life to individuals, and in reconciling divisions between people. The words of the service also emphasize that, as we receive the healing grace of God, so we are called to reach out in reconciling love to others, and to welcome them to share the blessings we enjoy. The fourth special service, which we have in mid-summer at Petertide, celebrates our shared ministry. Since the health of the community – in common with every Christian group – depends on all persons developing and using their particular spiritual gifts, every member is commissioned anew as a minister in Christ. This same service is also used from time to time when a particular person is commissioned as a pastor of the community.

The Sentences, Readings and Collects are for use during daily prayer and the weekly communion. The calendar follows the common tradition of most Western churches, except that an additional season, starting with the renewal of the covenant in early autumn, is put at the beginning. This has the effect of dividing the year into four equal parts, around four major festivals, and avoids the excessively large number of weeks to be counted after Pentecost. Each week has a theme, expressed in the opening Scripture sentence and the communion readings. These themes, apart from those during the festival weeks, are derived from the words of the four special services; the text on which the phrases of these services are based form the opening Scripture sentences. Thus the emphasis of the weekly themes is practical, rather than theological, reflecting the various aspects of Christian community life. However, one need not stick too closely to these themes: we frequently use other readings at the Communion service, depending on the subject of the talk being given.

Silence in worship is as important as words, and these services give ample opportunity for times of quiet. Yet it is easy to let the silence be eroded, especially if the group does not know how long to expect the silences to last. For this reason it can be helpful to agree on their approximate length – for example, two minutes after the readings in the Daily Prayer, three minutes for the confession during Communion, and so on. Also during the free prayer we should not be afraid of periods of quiet between the spoken prayers, and we should try to be quite brief in the prayers we say aloud. Rather than feeling that the times of silence interrupt the flow of words, we should regard the words of the service as rising out of our silent awareness of God's presence amongst us.

SERVICES

Daily Prayer

We pray in common once a day. Those able to do so come together in groups or as families, to support and sustain one another in prayer; others use the same form of worship on their own. In the course of our daily prayer we pray for each member of the community in turn.

The President reads the opening Scripture sentence.

PRAISING

President   With one voice we give praise to God.

People   To him be eternal glory.

There is a psalm from the Old Testament, then a psalm from the New Testament.

LISTENING

President   We proclaim the good news of God.

People   May his word dwell in our hearts.

There is a reading from the Old Testament, then a reading from the New Testament, followed by a time of silence.

PRAYING

President   Lord, teach us to pray.

People   Our Father in heaven, hallowed be your name, your kingdom come, your will be done, on earth as in heaven. Give us today our daily bread. Forgive us our sins, as we forgive those who sin against us. Lead us not into temptation, but deliver us from evil. For the kingdom, the power and the glory are yours, now and for ever. Amen.

Free prayer, concluding with the collect for the week.

BLESSING

President   Let us seek to follow the way of Christ in all we do.

People   May the grace of our Lord Jesus Christ, the love of God, and the fellowship of the Holy Spirit be with us all. Amen.

When this service is used by people on their own, it may be best to leave out the opening verses and responses of each section, yet retain the Lord's Prayer and the Grace.

Communion

Each week those who are able come together in groups to celebrate Communion. All members, from whatever Christian tradition they come, receive the bread and the wine; and children at the discretion of their parents also receive, as fellow members of Christ's family. If possible we also come together to share a meal each week.

An opening hymn may be sung. Then the President reads a seasonal Scripture sentence.

PREPARING

President Jesus said: 'Where two or three gather in my name, I am there with them.'

People **God invites us to the feast of his kingdom, calling us to be his holy people. We prepare ourselves by confessing our sins, and asking forgiveness.**

Silence

President God promises that those who turn from their sins shall be brought into perfect fellowship.

People **We greet one another in the love of Christ, praying that we and all God's people may live in peace.**

The People exchange a sign of peace. A hymn may be sung.

TEACHING

President Jesus said: 'The first commandment is this: love the Lord your God with all your heart, with all your soul, with all your mind, and with all your strength. The second is like it: love your neighbour as you love yourself.'

People **Put these your laws in our minds, and write them on our hearts.**

Reading and/or a talk.

President The Word of God is the source of life, and dwells among us.

People **We proclaim that Jesus Christ is Lord, to the glory of God the Father.**

A hymn may be sung.

OFFERING

President Jesus, our living hope, offered himself to the Father, praying: 'Not my will, but yours be done.'

People	**Our Father in heaven, hallowed be your name, your kingdom come, your will be done, on earth as in heaven. Give us today our daily bread. Forgive us our sins, as we forgive those who sin against us. Lead us not into temptation, but deliver us from evil. For the kingdom, the power and the glory are yours, now and for ever. Amen.**

Free prayer, concluding with the collect of the week.

President	God hears our prayers, and works for good in all things with those who love him.

People	**We offer ourselves as instruments of his righteousness in the world.**

The bread and wine are brought to the Lord's table.

A hymn may be sung.

CELEBRATING

President	Jesus prayed to the Father for his disciples, saying: 'May they be one, as you and I are one, that the world may know that you sent me.'

People	**Almighty God, through the sacrifice of your Son Jesus Christ, you have revealed for us the way of eternal life. Sanctify us in your truth, and set us free to serve you in humble praise.**

President	On the night that he was betrayed Jesus took bread, gave thanks to God, broke it and said: 'Take and eat. This is my body, which is given for you: do this in remembrance of me.' In the same way he took the cup and said: 'Drink this, all of you. This is my blood of the new covenant, which is shed for you and for many for the forgiveness of sins: do this, as often as you drink it, in remembrance of me.'

People	**Father, in obedience to your Son Jesus Christ, we celebrate with this bread and this cup his victory on the cross, lifting our hearts to you in joyful thanksgiving. We praise you for your whole creation, that through it we may see your glory;**

and we thank you that in Jesus Christ we die to
sin and are raised to new life.

President   God calls us to be a kingdom of priests, that the world
may know his wonderful power.

People   **May God fill us with his spirit of love, faith and
hope, that we may grow in the image of Christ.**

The President breaks the bread.

President   We break this bread to share in the body of Christ.

People   **Though we are many we are one body, because
we all share in one bread.**

*The bread and wine are shared. As the bread is given, the words 'The
body of Christ' may be said; and as the wine is given, the words 'The
blood of Christ' may be said. This may be followed by a time of silence.*

PROMISING

President   Jesus promised his disciples: 'I shall be with you always,
to the end of time. My Spirit will guide you in all
truth.'

People   **May we know by faith God's presence in our
lives.**

President   God sends us into the world to work as partners in his
kingdom.

People   **In the name of Christ. Amen.**

A hymn may be sung.

Covenant

Each year in early autumn we renew our covenant before God as members of the community; at the same service we also receive new members into the community. Before formally joining the community prospective members share for a period in its prayer and fellowship, seeking to discern, with the help of a pastor, whether their Christian discipleship would be strengthened through membership; when they and the pastor feel it is right, the pastor commends them to the community as members.

This service takes place during Communion, after the Teaching section.

President   As God has established a new covenant with his people in Jesus Christ, we pray that we may be seeds of his kingdom on earth.

People   **We commit ourselves to one another as fellow disciples of Christ, worshipping him together in prayer and in action.**

President   God binds us together in mutual trust, that we may support one another through warm and tender friendship.

People   **May we be loyal and steadfast partners in his service, cherishing one another both in sorrow and in joy.**

President   God has made us members one of another with Christ as our head, that we may be joined together in common vision and purpose.

People   **May we receive graciously into our midst those whom God sends, growing as one body in his love.**

Everyone stands in a circle.

President   God's covenant with his people is written by his Spirit on our hearts, that we may live in union with him.

If any people are to join the community, the President takes each new member by the hand, and everyone says together:

People   **N, we thank God for you, and we joyfully acknowledge you as brother/sister in his name, to his glory and honour.**

Everyone joins hands, saying together:

People   **We thank God for each other, and we joyfully acknowledge one another as brothers and sisters in his name, to his glory and honour.**

A hymn may be sung.

Stewardship

Each year during the Christmas season we commit anew our time and resources to God's service. Beforehand all members speak in confidence with a pastor reviewing their stewardship, seeking in their use of time to find the right balance between prayer, work and leisure; and in their use of money and other material resources the right balance between the claims of family, community, local church, and the poor and deprived of the world.

This service takes place during Communion, after the Teaching section.

President   As God in Christ teaches his people to be faithful
             stewards of his creation, we pray that through our work
             and fellowship we may bear a rich harvest of love.

People   **We offer all that we have to be used in his service,
             asking that we may each receive according to our
             needs.**

President   God has called us into a loving family of faith, that we
             may find joy in sharing his rich blessings.

People   **Let us be compassionate and sensitive to the
             needs of others, devoting ourselves with cheerful
             and willing hearts to the good of all.**

President   God provides us each with many gifts, that we may be
             generous in our mutual care.

People   **Let us be honest and thoughtful in using our
             talents and resources, performing with diligence
             the tasks given to us.**

*The People come to the Lord's Table, kneel, and put on or beside it a
token of what they are able to share with others, perhaps an object
symbolizing some aspect of their work. Children may bring toys.*

President   God in Christ makes his home in our hearts, that we
             may glorify him in all that we do.

People   **We kneel and worship our Lord and Saviour,
             giving back to him what he has given to us.**

A hymn may be sung.

Reconciliation

Each year during Lent, and at other times if it seems necessary, we have a service of reconciliation. Beforehand we each find time for personal reflection, perhaps with the confidential counsel of a pastor, seeking to discern those aspects of our lives where we are not at peace with God and with other people.

This service takes place during Communion, after the Teaching section.

President As God through the death and resurrection of his Son has reconciled mankind to himself, we pray that we may grow and mature in the image of the risen Christ.

People **We seek to live in harmony with one another, bearing witness to the peace to which all people are called.**

President God is infinitely patient in his desire for us to repent, that we in turn may be tolerant and compassionate.

People **May we be slow to judge the sins of others and quick to confess our own, forgiving others as Christ forgives us.**

President God in his mercy makes us whole, that we who are weak and foolish may proclaim his power and wisdom.

People **May we always be ready to open our hearts to others, reaching out to all we meet with the hand of his love.**

The President and another person lay hands on those who wish to receive a sign of God's reconciling love. They begin by laying hands on one another. As the sign is made, the President may say, 'May Almighty God make you whole in body, mind and spirit, according to his will', and the person receiving the sign may say, 'Amen'. When all who wish have received the sign, the following words are spoken:

President By the wounds of Christ we are made whole, that we may show forth his glory in the world.

People **May we live in union with him, in all things giving thanks to God.**

A hymn may be sung.

Ministry

Each year during the Pentecost season we reaffirm all the members of the community as ministers of Christ, recognizing that we all have spiritual gifts from God to be used within and outside the community. Also from time to time we commission particular people as pastors to guide us in our discipleship. Pastors are chosen with the unanimous consent of the community, as people sensitive to the needs and insights of others, yet resolute and clear-sighted in leadership.

This service takes place during Communion, after the Teaching section.

President   As God in Christ came to minister to people in all their needs, we pray that we may be fellow-servants rooted and grounded in his self-giving love.

People   **We strive to order our lives in obedience to God's will, supporting one another in our various vocations.**

President   God in his Spirit reveals the truth as we need, that we may guide each other in the way of Christ.

People   **May we listen to one another with deference, striving to discern and express what is right for all.**

President   God in Jesus has given us the perfect master, that we may commission others under his power to lead his people.

People   **May we each exercise with humility and courage such authority as is vested in us, rejoicing in the wise counsel that others may give.**

The President with another person lays hands on each of those being commissioned, during which the following words are spoken:

President   N, God has commissioned you as his servant. Guard the vision entrusted to you. Hold fast to what is good, and reject what is evil.

People   **May we receive your ministry with thankfulness, and support you in prayerful love.**

A hymn may be sung.

SENTENCES, READINGS AND COLLECTS

The calendar begins in early autumn with the Covenant renewal. Covenant week starts on the Seventeenth Sunday before Christmas, which is the Sunday falling between 28th August and 3rd September inclusive. The Covenant service itself may take place at the beginning of the week, or on the following Saturday evening or on Sunday.

An adjustment will often need to be made to the calendar according to the date of Easter. If the Seventh Sunday before Easter (i.e. immediately preceding Ash Wednesday) occurs before Christmas 9 is completed, the sentences, readings and collects for the remaining weeks of the Christmas season should be added to the Pentecost season, until Covenant week is reached. If the Seventh Sunday before Easter occurs after the end of Christmas 9, the sentences, readings and collects from the end of the Pentecost season should be added to the end of the Christmas season.

The cycle of Bible readings covers two years. The readings for Year 1 should be used when the Covenant service falls in an odd-numbered year, and for Year 2 when it falls in an even-numbered year. The readings for Sunday are for the weekly Communion service, and the weekday readings are for the Daily Prayer.

In addition to the major festivals there are eighteen minor festivals for which special psalms and readings are given. Most of these are listed separately at the end of this section, but those which fall in a regular place in the calendar are shown accordingly.

COVENANT WEEK

All whom the Father gives me will come to me, and the person who comes to me I will never turn away.

from John 6

Day	Psalm	Year 1	Year 2
S		Ezek 37.15–end John 6.35–40	Jer 31.31–37 1 John 1.1–4
M	1	Gen 9.1–17 1 Pet 3.13–end	Gen 9.1–17 1 Pet 3.13–end
T	13	Gen 17.1–7 Gal 4.21–end	Gen 17.1–7 Gal 4.21–end
W	25	Deut 4.9–13 Heb 12.18–end	Deut 4.9–13 Heb 12.18–end
Th	37	2 Chron 5.2—6.2 2 Cor 2.14—3.6	2 Chron 5.2—6.2 2 Cor 2.14—3.6
F	49	Neh 1 Heb 8.1–6	Neh 1 Heb 8.1–6
S	61	Dan 1.1–19 Acts 3.11–end	Dan 1.1–19 Acts 3.11–end

O Lord, you lead all who keep your covenant in faithfulness and love. Show us your ways and guide us in your truth, for you are the God of our salvation.

from Psalm 25

COVENANT 1

Christ is the mediator of the new covenant, that we may be set free
from our sins and receive God's eternal blessings.

from Hebrews 9

Day	Psalm	Year 1	Year 2
S		1 Sam 15.10–23	Deut 10.12–end
		John 14.15–26	Heb 9.11–15
M	1	Gen 1.1–19	Exod 1
		Matt 4.1–11	John 1.1–18
T	2	Gen 1.20—2.3	Exod 2.1–10
		Matt 4.12–22	John 1.19–28
W	3	Gen 2.4–end	Exod 2.11–end
		Matt 4.23—5.12	John 1.29–34
Th	4	Gen 3.1–13	Exod 3.1–12
		Matt 5.13–20	John 1.35–end
F	5	Gen 3.14–end	Exod 3.13–end
		Matt 5.21–26	John 2.1–12
S	6	Gen 4.1–16	Exod 4.1–17
		Matt 5.27–37	John 2.13–end

Lord, you have set your people free, and made an eternal
covenant with them. Give us wisdom to honour you, and sound
judgement to keep your commandments.

from Psalm 111

COVENANT 2

The Son of Man sows the good seed; his field is the world, and the good seed is the people who belong to the kingdom.

from Matthew 13

Day	Psalm	Year 1	Year 2
S		Isa 32 1 Pet 1.13–end	Isa 30.19–26 Matt 13.24–30, 36–43
M	7	Gen 6.5–end Matt 5.38–end	Exod 4.18–end John 3.1–13
T	8	Gen 7 Matt 6.1–18	Exod 5.1–14 John 3.14–21
W	9	Gen 8 Matt 6.19–end	Exod 5.15—6.1 John 3.22–end
Th	10	Gen 9.1–17 Matt 7.1–12	Exod 7.8–end John 4.1–15
F	11	Gen 11.1–9 Matt 7.13–end	Exod 11 John 4.16–26
S	12	Gen 11.27—12.9 Matt 8.1–13	Exod 12.1–20 John 4.27–42

We pray that the sharing of our faith may deepen our understanding of the blessings which are ours in Christ; and that through our brotherhood in him God's people may be renewed.

from Philemon

COVENANT 3

By this shall all men know that you are my disciples, that you have love for one another.

from John 13

Day	Psalm	Year 1	Year 2
S		Jer 32.36–41 John 13.31–35	Exod 19.1–8 Phil 2.1–18
M	13	Gen 12.10–end Matt 8.14–22	Exod 12.21–36 John 4.43–end
T	14	Gen 13 Matt 8.23–end	Exod 12.37–end John 5.1–18
W	15	Gen 14.1–16 Matt 9.1–13	Exod 13.1–16 John 5.19–29
Th	16	Gen 14.17–end Matt 9.14–26	Exod 13.17–end John 5.30–end
F	17	Gen 16 Matt 9.27–end	Exod 14.1–14 John 6.1–15
S	18	Gen 17.1–22 Matt 10.1–15	Exod 14.15–end John 6.16–29

O God, we pray that you will draw us together in love, to have the riches of complete understanding of your mystery, which is Christ himself.

from Colossians 2

Day after day they met in the temple, praising God and enjoying the good will of all people.

from Acts 2

Day	Psalm	Year 1	Year 2
S		Isa 55.1–11 Acts 2.38–end	Dan 12.1–3 Matt 25.31–end
M	19	Gen 18.1–15 Matt 10.16–33	Exod 15.1–21 John 6.30–40
T	20	Gen 18.16–end Matt 10.34–end	Exod 15.22–end John 6.41–51
W	21	Gen 19.1–11 Matt 11.1–19	Exod 16.1–18 John 6.52–59
Th	22	Gen 19.12–29 Matt 11.20–end	Exod 16.19–end John 6.60–end
F	23	Gen 20 Matt 12.1–21	Exod 17 John 7.1–13
S	24	Gen 21.1–21 Matt 12.22–37	Exod 18.1–12 John 7.14–24

O Lord, you are exalted above the heavens, and your glory is over all the earth. Awaken our souls, and fix our hearts upon you, that we may praise you among all people.

from Psalm 57

COVENANT 5

Whoever can be trusted in small things can be trusted also in great.

from Luke 16

Day	Psalm	Year 1	Year 2
S		Isa 45.1–19 Luke 16.1–12	Isa 49.8–13 2 Cor 6.1–13
M	25	Gen 22.1–19 Matt 12.38–end	Exod 18.13–end John 7.25–31
T	26	Gen 23 Matt 13.1–9	Exod 19.1—15 John 7.32–39
W	27	Gen 24.1–14 Matt 13.10–23	Exod 19.16–end John 7.40–end
Th	28	Gen 24.15–28 Matt 13.24–33	Exod 20.1–17 John 8.1–11
F	29	Gen 24.29–49 Matt 13.34–43	Exod 20.18–24 John 8.12–20
S	30	Gen 24.50–end Matt 13.44–end	Exod 23.1–17 John 8.21–30

O Lord, the earth is filled with your loving kindness, and you watch over those who put their trust in you. May our hearts rejoice in you, and your constant love be upon us.

from Psalm 33

COVENANT 6

This is my commandment, that you love one another as I have loved you. You are my friends if you do what I command you.

from John 15

Day	Psalm	Year 1	Year 2
S		Isa 26.1–12 2 Cor 11.16–end	1 Chron 29.10–20 John 15.12–17
M	31	Gen 25.7–11, 19–end Matt 14.1–12	Exod 24 John 8.31–47
T	32	Gen 26.1–15 Matt 14.13–end	Exod 32.1–10 John 8.48–end
W	33	Gen 26.16–33 Matt 15.1–20	Exod 32.11–24 John 9.1–12
Th	34	Gen 27.1–17 Matt 15.21–28	Exod 32.25–end John 9.13–23
F	35	Gen 27.18–29 Matt 15.29–end	Exod 33.1–11 John 9.24–end
S	36	Gen 27.30–40 Matt 16.1–12	Exod 33.12–end John 10.1–10

Father, you have called us into the fellowship of your Son. Keep us faithful and faultless to the end, when Jesus Christ our Lord shall be revealed.

from 1 Corinthians 1

COVENANT 7

We are partners working together for God in his field, each doing
the work God gives him to do.

from 1 Corinthians 3

Day	Psalm	Year 1	Year 2
S		Eccl 3.1–13 Luke 20.1–18	Isa 40.1–11 1 Cor 3.1–9
M	37	Gen 27.41—28.9 Matt 16.13–end	Exod 34.1–10, 29–end John 10.11–21
T	38	Gen 28.10–end Matt 17.1–13	Exod 35.20—36.7 John 10.22–end
W	39	Gen 29.1–14 Matt 17.14–21	Exod 40.1–15 John 11.1–16
Th	40	Gen 29.15–30 Matt 17.22–end	Exod 40.16–end John 11.17–27
F	41	Gen 31.1–21 Matt 18.1–20	Lev 25.1–7, 20–22 John 11.28–37
S	42	Gen 32.3–21 Matt 18.21–end	Lev 25.8–17 John 11.38–44

With joy we give thanks to the Father, who through his beloved
Son has set us free from our sins, delivering us from darkness to his
kingdom of light.

from Colossians 1

COVENANT 8

Rejoice with those who rejoice, weep with those who weep.

from Romans 12

Day	Psalm	Year 1	Year 2
S		Isa 25.6–9 Rom 12.14–end	Job 3.2–end Matt 16.21–end
M	43	Gen 32.22–end Matt 19.1–15	Lev 25.23–34 John 11.45–end
T	44	Gen 33.1–17 Matt 19.16–end	Lev 25.35–46 John 12.1–11
W	45	Gen 34.1–24 Matt 20.1–16	Lev 25.47–end John 12.12–19
Th	46	Gen 34.25–end Matt 20.17–end	Deut 4.1–14 John 12.20–26
F	47	Gen 35.1–15 Matt 21.1–17	Deut 4.15–31 John 12.27–36
S	48	Gen 35.16–end Matt 21.18–32	Deut 4.32–40 John 12.37–end

O God, whose righteousness reaches to the heavens, you have burdened us with many and bitter troubles. Turn and renew us, raising us up from the depths of the earth.

from Psalm 71

COVENANT 9

Let us put away falsehood and speak the truth, for we are members one of another.

from Ephesians 3

Day	Psalm	Year 1	Year 2
S		1 Sam 20.1–17 Matt 11.25–end	Jer 31.7–14 Eph 4.17–end
M	49	Gen 37.1–11 Matt 21.33–end	Deut 6.1–9 John 13.1–11
T	50	Gen 37.12–end Matt 22.1–14	Deut 6.10–end John 13.12–20
W	51	Gen 39 Matt 22.15–33	Deut 8.1–10 John 13.21–30
Th	52	Gen 40 Matt 22.34–end	Deut 8.11–end John 13.31–end
F	53	Gen 41.1–16 Matt 23.1–15	Deut 10.12–end John 14.1–14
S	54	Gen 41.17–36 Matt 23.16–28	Deut 11.18–end John 14.15–end

Lord, you never abandon us, but stay close beside us. Have mercy upon us when we are weak, and heal us when we are afraid.

from Psalm 6

COVENANT 10

We are joined together as members of one body, with all the different parts having the same care for one another.

from 1 Corinthians 12

Day	Psalm	Year 1	Year 2
S		Isa 57.14–19 Eph 4.1–16	Mic 4.1–4 John 14.27–31
M	55	Gen 41.37–end Matt 23.29–end	Deut 12.1–14 John 15.1–17
T	56	Gen 42.1–24 Matt 24.1–14	Deut 17.14–end John 15.18–end
W	57	Gen 42.25–end Matt 24.15–28	Deut 18.1–13 John 16.1–15
Th	58	Gen 43.1–14 Matt 24.29–end	Deut 18.14–end John 16.16–24
F	59	Gen 43.15–end Matt 25.1–13	Deut 19.1–13 John 16.25–end
S	60	Gen 44.1–17 Matt 25.14–30	Deut 24.10–end John 17.1–8

O Lord, bless us and keep us; make your face shine upon us and be gracious to us; look upon us with favour and give us your peace.

from Numbers 6

COVENANT 11

Accept one another as Christ has accepted you, for the glory of God.

from Romans 15

Day	Psalm	Year 1	Year 2
S		1 Sam 3.1–18 Mark 1.14–20	1 Sam 2.1–10 Rom 15.1–7
M	61	Gen 44.18–end Matt 25.31–end	Deut 26.1–15 John 17.9–end
T	62	Gen 45.1–15 Matt 26.1–13	Deut 30.1–10 John 18.1–11
W	63	Gen 45.16–end Matt 26.14–29	Deut 30.11–end John 18.12–27
Th	64	Gen 46.1–7, 28–end Matt 26.30–46	Deut 31.1–8 John 18.28–end
F	65	Gen 47.1–12 Matt 26.47–56	Deut 31.14–29 John 19.1–16
S	66	Gen 47.13–end Matt 26.57–end	Deut 31.30—32.14 John 19.17–27

We pray to the Father, from whom every family in heaven and on earth receives its true name, that Christ may find a home in our hearts, and that through his Spirit we may grow in spiritual strength.

from Ephesians 3

COVENANT 12

Faith, hope and love abide, these three; but the greatest of these is love.

from 1 Corinthians 13

Day	Psalm	Year 1	Year 2
S		Jer 10.1–10 1 Cor 12.1–13	Dan 4.34–end John 4.5–26
M	67	Gen 48.1–12 Matt 27.1–10	Deut 32.15–27 John 19.28–end
T	68	Gen 48.13–end Matt 27.11–26	Deut 32.28–43 John 20.1–10
W	69	Gen 49.1–13 Matt 27.27–44	Deut 33.1–11 John 20.11–23
Th	70	Gen 49.14–28 Matt 27.45–56	Deut 33.12–21 John 20.24–end
F	71	Gen 49.29—50.14 Matt 27.57–end	Deut 33.22–end John 21.1–14
S	72	Gen 50.15–end Matt 28	Deut 34 John 21.15–end

We give you thanks, O God, for the joy we receive in your presence. May you enable our love for one another to grow in abundance, that our hearts may be perfect in holiness at the coming of our Lord Jesus Christ.

from 1 Thessalonians 3

ADVENT 1

Be good stewards of God's varied gifts, so that in all things you may give praise to him.

from 1 Peter 4

Day	Psalm	Year 1	Year 2
S		Deut 1.9–17 Matt 25.14–30	1 Kings 3.6–14 1 Pet 4.7–11
M	1	Isa 1.1–14 1 Thess 1	Ezek 1.1–14 2 Thess 1
T	2	Isa 1.15–end 1 Thess 2.1–12	Ezek 1.15–end 2 Thess 2
W	3	Isa 3.1–15 1 Thess 2.13–end	Ezek 2.1—3.3 2 Thess 3
Th	4	Isa 4.2—5.7 1 Thess 3	Ezek 3.4–15 1 John 1
F	5	Isa 5.8–24 1 Thess 4	Ezek 3.16–end 1 John 2.1–14
S	6	Isa 5.25–end 1 Thess 5	Ezek 4 1 John 2.15–end

O Lord, our governor, your glory is seen in all the earth. You made us little less than gods, crowning us with glory and honour. Make us worthy masters of your handiwork.

from Psalm 8

ADVENT 2

Let us love one another, because love comes from God. Whoever loves is a child of God and knows God.

from 1 John 4

Day	Psalm	Year 1	Year 2
S		Deut 6.1–9 1 John 4.7–end	Ezek 16.1–14 Matt 5.3–12
M	7	Isa 6 2 John	Ezek 5 1 John 3.1–10
T	8	Isa 7.1–9 3 John	Ezek 12.1–16 1 John 3.11–end
W	9	Isa 7.10–end Luke 1.1–17	Ezek 12.17–end 1 John 4.1–6
Th	10	Isa 9.2–7 Luke 1.18–25	Ezek 17.22—18.13 1 John 4.7–end
F	11	Isa 11.1–9 Luke 1.26–38	Ezek 24.15–end 1 John 5
S	12	Isa 12 Luke 1.39–56	Ezek 33.10–20 2 Pet 1.1–15

We pray that we may be rooted and grounded in love, that we may know the breadth and length, the height and depth of the love of Christ, and be filled with the very nature of God himself.

from Ephesians 3

ADVENT 3

This is the true worship that you should offer to God: to do what is good and pleasing to him.

from Romans 12

Day	Psalm	Year 1	Year 2
S		Zech 7.4–10	Gen 12.1–9
		Luke 19.1–10	Rom 12.1–8
M	13	Isa 24	Ezek 33.11–22
		Luke 1.57–66	2 Pet 1.16—2.3
T	14	Isa 26.1–13	Ezek 33.23–end
		Luke 1.67–end	2 Pet 2.4–end
W	15	Isa 28.1–13	Ezek 36.1–15
		Luke 2.1–21	2 Pet 3
Th	16	Isa 28.14–end	Ezek 36.22–36
		Luke 2.22–end	Matt 1.18—2.12
F	17	Isa 33.1–16	Ezek 37.1–14
		Luke 3.1–14	Matt 2.13–end
S	18	Isa 35	Ezek 47.1–12
		Luke 3.15–23	Matt 3

Lord, you are all-powerful, and no purpose of yours can be thwarted. Your works are beyond our understanding, and your marvels too great for us to know. May we listen when you speak and respond to your commands.

from Job 42

CHRISTMAS WEEK

I bring you good news of great joy: to you is born in the city of
David a Saviour who is Christ the Lord.

from Luke 2

Day	Psalm	Year 1	Year 2
S		Deut 32.39–43 Heb 1.1–6	Isa 11.1–9 John 6.25–34
M	8	1 Chron 17.1–14 Titus 2.11–14	1 Chron 17.1–14 Titus 2.11–14
T	20	1 Sam 16.1–13 Acts 13.16–26	1 Sam 16.1–13 Acts 13.16–26
W	32	Isa 63.15—64 end Rom 1.1–7	Isa 63.15—64 end Rom 1.1–7
Th	44	Isa 44.21–26 1 Cor 1.26–end	Isa 44.21–26 1 Cor 1.26–end
F	56	Isa 62.1–5 2 Cor 8.1–9	Isa 62.1–5 2 Cor 8.1–9
S	68	Lev 26.1–13 Rev 21.1–7	Lev 26.1–13 Rev 21.1–7
		CHRISTMAS COMMUNION Isa 62.10–12 Luke 2.1–20	Mic 5.2–5a Matt 1.18–end

Eternal God, you have given us your Son to be our king. May
he rule over the nations with justice and with righteousness, that all
mankind may live in peace.

from Isaiah 9

CHRISTMAS 1

The believers were united in heart and soul, distributing their wealth
to each according to need.

from Acts 4

Day	Psalm	Year 1	Year 2
S		Deut 15.1–11 Acts 4.32—5.11	Lev 25.8–17 Luke 12.16–21
M	19	Josh 1.1–11 Mark 1.1–13	2 Sam 1.1–16 1 Cor 1.1–17
T	20	Josh 2.1–13 Mark 1.14–28	2 Sam 1.17–end 1 Cor 1.18–end
W	21	Josh 2.14–end Mark 1.29–end	2 Sam 2.1–11 1 Cor 2
Th	22	Josh 3 Mark 2.1–12	2 Sam 2.12–end 1 Cor 3
F	23	Josh 6.1–16 Mark 2.13–22	2 Sam 5.1–10 1 Cor 4
S	24	Josh 6.17–end Mark 2.23—3.6	2 Sam 6.1–11 1 Cor 5

Lord, you do not forget the weak and the poor, but help and redeem
them. May all who seek you find joy and gladness.

from Psalm 70

We have been taught by our fellowship in the Lord Jesus to love one another as brothers.

from 1 Thessalonians 4

Day	Psalm	Year 1	Year 2
S		Hos 2.14–end Mark 10.2–16	2 Sam 22.26–end 1 Thess 4.1–12
M	25	Judg 2.6–end Mark 3.7–19	2 Sam 6.12–end 1 Cor 6.1–11
T	26	Judg 4.1–16 Mark 3.20–end	2 Sam 7.1–17 1 Cor 6.12–end
W	27	Judg 4.17–end Mark 4.1–20	2 Sam 7.18–end 1 Cor 7.1–24
Th	28	Judg 6.1, 11–24 Mark 4.21–34	2 Sam 9 1 Cor 7.25–end
F	29	Judg 6.25–end Mark 4.35–end	2 Sam 11.1–13 1 Cor 8
S	30	Judg 7.1–15 Mark 5.1–20	2 Sam 11.14–end 1 Cor 9.1–14

Lord, fill us with courage: in you we have nothing to fear, for you answer our every prayer. Let your blessings be upon all your people.

from Psalm 3

CHRISTMAS 3

Give glory to God through sharing with others the rich blessings
you have received from him.

from 2 Corinthians 9

Day	Psalm	Year 1	Year 2
S		Isa 40.25–end 2 Cor 9.6–end	Jer 16.19–end Matt 15.21–31
M	31	Judg 7.16–end Mark 5.21–34	2 Sam 12.1–14 1 Cor 9.15–end
T	32	Judg 13.1–7 Mark 5.35–end	2 Sam 12.15–25 1 Cor 10.1–13
W	33	Judg 13.8–end Mark 6.1–13	2 Sam 15.1–12 1 Cor 10.14—11.1
Th	34	Judg 14.1–11 Mark 6.14–29	2 Sam 15.13–29 1 Cor 11.2–16
F	35	Judg 14.12–end Mark 6.30–44	2 Sam 15.30—16.4 1 Cor 11.17–end
S	36	Judg 15.1–8 Mark 6.45–end	2 Sam 16.5–14 1 Cor 12.1–11

We give thanks to God for the grace he has given us in Christ Jesus,
that in union with him we have become rich in every spiritual gift.

from 1 Corinthians 1

Be one in thought and feeling, full of brotherly love, with tender hearts and humble minds.

from 1 Peter 3

Day	Psalm	Year 1	Year 2
S		Zeph 3.14–end Mark 3.20–end	Mic 6.6–15 1 Pet 3.8–12
M	37	Judg 15.9–end Mark 7.1–13	2 Sam 17.1–14 1 Cor 12.12–end
T	38	Judg 16.1–22 Mark 7.14–23	2 Sam 18.1–18 1 Cor 13
W	39	Judg 16.23–end Mark 7.24–end	2 Sam 18.19–end 1 Cor 14.1–12
Th	40	1 Sam 1.1–18 Mark 8.1–10	2 Sam 19.1–8a 1 Cor 14.13–25
F	41	1 Sam 1.19–end Mark 8.11–21	2 Sam 19.24–39 1 Cor 14.26–end
S	42	1 Sam 2.1–11 Mark 8.22–30	1 Kings 1.1–10 1 Cor 15.1–11

Lord, your law is perfect, giving us strength, and your commands are true, making us wise. May the words of our mouths and the meditations of our hearts be acceptable in your sight.

from Psalm 19

CHRISTMAS 5

Do not grow weary of serving others, but work quietly and diligently in the name of the Lord Jesus.

from 2 Thessalonians 3

Day	Psalm	Year 1	Year 2
S		Lev 25.1–7 2 Thess 3.6–13	2 Chron 9.1–8 Matt 20.1–16
M	43	1 Sam 3.1–19 Mark 8.31—9.1	1 Kings 1.11–27 1 Cor 15.12–34
T	44	1 Sam 4.1–11 Mark 9.2–13	1 Kings 1.28–40 1 Cor 15.35–49
W	45	1 Sam 4.12–18 Mark 9.14–29	1 Kings 1.41–end 1 Cor 15.50–end
Th	46	1 Sam 5 Mark 9.30–37	1 Kings 2.1–12 1 Cor 16
F	47	1 Sam 6.1–12 Mark 9.38–end	1 Kings 3.1–15 2 Cor 1.1–14
S	48	1 Sam 8 Mark 10.1–16	1 Kings 3.16–end 2 Cor 1.15—2.4

We give thanks to God, the Father of our Lord Jesus Christ, that, just as we have learnt through the gospel the riches of his blessings, so the gospel continues to spread throughout the world.

from Colossians 1

CHRISTMAS 6

Seek first the kingdom of God and his justice, and all you need will be yours as well.

from Matthew 6

Day	Psalm	Year 1	Year 2
S		Amos 5.10–24 Matt 6.24–end	Isa 42.1–7 1 Tim 6.6–19
M	49	1 Sam 9.1–14 Mark 10.17–31	1 Kings 5.1–12 2 Cor 2.5–end
T	50	1 Sam 9.15–end Mark 10.32–34	1 Kings 8.1–13 2 Cor 3
W	51	1 Sam 10.1–16 Mark 10.35–45	1 Kings 8.14–30 2 Cor 4
Th	52	1 Sam 10.17–end Mark 10.46–end	1 Kings 10.1–13 2 Cor 5
F	53	1 Sam 11.1–12 Mark 11.1–11	1 Kings 10.14–25 2 Cor 6.1–13
S	54	1 Sam 11.13–end Mark 11.12–26	1 Kings 11.1–13 2 Cor 6.14—7.1

O Lord most high, who are the judge of all mankind, we thank and praise you for your justice. May you gather all peoples about you, and rule over them.

from Psalm 7

CHRISTMAS 7

Give generously to others, as you have received.

from Matthew 10

Day	Psalm	Year 1	Year 2
S		Lev 19.9–18 2 Cor 8.1–15	1 Chron 29.1–9 Matt 10.5–15
M	55	1 Sam 13.1–14 Mark 11.27–end	1 Kings 11.41—12.17 2 Cor 7.2–end
T	56	1 Sam 14.1–15 Mark 12.1–12	1 Kings 16.29—17.7 2 Cor 8.1–15
W	57	1 Sam 14.24–35 Mark 12.13–27	1 Kings 17.8–end 2 Cor 8.16—9.5
Th	58	1 Sam 14.36–46 Mark 12.28–34	1 Kings 18.1–19 2 Cor 9.6–end
F	59	1 Sam 15.1–9 Mark 12.35–end	1 Kings 18.20–29 2 Cor 10
S	60	1 Sam 15.10–23 Mark 13.1–13	1 Kings 18.30–end 2 Cor 11.1–15

Blessed be our God and Father, the source of all mercy. Help us in our troubles, that we in turn may give help to others.

from 2 Corinthians 1

CHRISTMAS 8

Bear one another's burdens in obedience to the law of Christ; and as opportunity arises do good to all people.

from Galatians 6

Day	Psalm	Year 1	Year 2
S		Zech 8.14–19 Luke 19.11–27	Ezek 18.5–9 Gal 6.1–10
M	61	1 Sam 16.1–13 Mark 13.14–27	1 Kings 19 2 Cor 11.16–end
T	62	1 Sam 16.14–end Mark 13.28–end	1 Kings 21.1–16 2 Cor 12
W	63	1 Sam 17.1–11 Mark 14.1–11	1 Kings 21.17–end 2 Cor 13
Th	64	1 Sam 17.12–25 Mark 14.12–26	2 Kings 2.1–15 Gal 1
F	65	1 Sam 17.26–40 Mark 14.27–42	2 Kings 4.1–7 Gal 2.1–10
S	66	1 Sam 17.41–54 Mark 14.43–52	2 Kings 5.1–14 Gal 2.11–end

Almighty God, you test men justly, and search out their hearts and minds. We put ourselves in your hands, knowing that your power will prevail.

from Jeremiah 20

CHRISTMAS 9

Whatever you are doing, put your whole heart into it, as if you were working for the Lord.

from Colossians 3

Day	Psalm	Year 1	Year 2
S		Ruth 1.6–18 Col 3.18—4.6	Exod 33.12–end Luke 6.46–end
M	67	1 Sam 17.55—18.16 Mark 14.53–65	2 Kings 5.15–end Gal 3.1–14
T	68	1 Sam 19.1–18 Mark 14.66–end	Ruth 1 Gal 3.15–end
W	69	1 Sam 20.1–17 Mark 15.1–15	Ruth 2.1–13 Gal 4.1–20
Th	70	1 Sam 20.18–end Mark 15.16–32	Ruth 2.14–end Gal 4.21—5.1
F	71	1 Sam 26 Mark 15.33–end	Ruth 3 Gal 5.2–end
S	72	1 Sam 31 Mark 16	Ruth 4.1–17 Gal 6

We give thanks to Christ Jesus our Lord for calling us to serve him, and for giving us strength for our work.

from 1 Timothy 1

7 BEFORE EASTER

While we were still enemies God reconciled us to himself through the death of his Son Jesus Christ.

from Romans 5

Day	Psalm	Year 1	Year 2
S		Exod 6.2–13 John 8.31–36	Exod 14.5–end Rom 5.1–11
M	1	Isa 40.1–11 Heb 1	Jer 1.1–10 Rom 1.1–7
T	2	Isa 40.12–26 Heb 2.1–9	Jer 1.11–end Rom 1.8–17
W	3	ASH WEDNESDAY Gen 3.1–13 Matt 4.1–11	Gen 4.1–16 Luke 4.1–13
Th	4	Isa 40.27—41.7 Heb 2.10–end	Jer 2.1–13 Rom 1.18–end
F	5	Isa 41.8–20 Heb 3	Jer 2.14–25 Rom 2.1–16
S	6	Isa 41.21–end Heb 4.1–13	Jer 2.26–end Rom 2.17–end

O Lord, whose word we praise, deliver us from death and keep us from falling. May we walk in your presence in the light of the living.

from Psalm 56

LENT 1

All of us reflect the glory of the Lord, and are transfigured into his likeness by the power of his Spirit.

from 2 Corinthians 3

Day	Psalm	Year 1	Year 2
S		Exod 34.29–end 2 Cor 3.13–end	Isa 35.1–10 John 11.1–4, 17–44
M	7	Isa 42.1–14 Heb 4.14—5 end	Jer 3.1–5 Rom 3.1–20
T	8	Isa 42.13–end Heb 6	Jer 3.6–18 Rom 3.21–end
W	9	Isa 43.1–13 Heb 7.1–10	Jer 4.1–14 Rom 4.1–12
Th	10	Isa 43.14–end Heb 7.11–end	Jer 5.1–11 Rom 4.13–end
F	11	Isa 44.1–8 Heb 8	Jer 7.1–15 Rom 5.1–11
S	12	Isa 44.21–end Heb 9.1–14	Jer 7.16–28 Rom 5.12–end

O God, from you alone come wisdom and understanding. You reveal deep mysteries, you know what lies in darkness, and the light dwells with you. We thank you for giving us wisdom and strength, and for making things known as we need.

from Daniel 2

LENT 2

Be at peace among yourselves. Do not repay evil with evil, but always seek to do good to one another.

from 1 Thessalonians 5

Day	Psalm	Year 1	Year 2
S		Jer 33.1–9 Matt 18.15–end	Mal 2.5–7 1 Thess 5.12–26
M	13	Isa 45.1–8 Heb 9.15–end	Jer 8.18—9.3 Rom 6.1–14
T	14	Isa 45.9–19 Heb 10.1–10	Jer 9.17–24 Rom 6.15–end
W	15	Isa 45.20–end Heb 10.11–25	Jer 10.1–16 Rom 7.1–6
Th	16	Isa 46 Heb 10.26–end	Jer 11.1–17 Rom 7.7–13
F	17	Isa 47 Heb 11.1–16	Jer 12.1–6 Rom 7.14–end
S	18	Isa 48.1–11 Heb 11.17–31	Jer 15.10–end Rom 8.1–17

O Lord, we thank you for the sweet fellowship we enjoy in your house. You hear our prayers and you bring peace to our souls. May we cast all our burdens upon you, for you will sustain us.

from Psalm 55

LENT 3

Peace I leave with you; my peace I give to you.

from John 14

Day	Psalm	Year 1	Year 2
S		Prov 16.1–7 Phil 4.4–9	Zech 3.6–10 John 14.27–31a
M	19	Isa 48.12–end Heb 11.32–end	Jer 16.1–13 Rom 8.18–30
T	20	Isa 49.1–7 Heb 12.1–13	Jer 20.7–end Rom 8.31–end
W	21	Isa 49.8–18 Heb 12.14–end	Jer 26.1–16 Rom 9.1–18
Th	22	Isa 49.19—50.3 Heb 13	Jer 29.1–14 Rom 9.19–29
F	23	Isa 50.4–end 1 Pet 1.1–12	Jer 30.1–11 Rom 9.30—10.13
S	24	Isa 51.1–11 1 Pet 1.13–end	Jer 30.12–22 Rom 10.14—11.10

Lord, you raise the lowly from the dust, and lift the poor from their misery. May you rule over the nations, and from the rising of the sun to its setting may your name be praised.

from Psalm 113

LENT 4

God is patient, because he wants all to turn away from their sins.

from 2 Peter 3

Day	Psalm	Year 1	Year 2
S		1 Sam 8 Luke 13.31–end	Gen 2.4b–end 2 Pet 3.2–13
M	25	Isa 51.12–end 1 Pet 2.1–10	Jer 31.7–14 Rom 11.11–24
T	26	Isa 52.1–12 1 Pet 2.11–end	Jer 31.15–22 Rom 11.25–end
W	27	Isa 52.13—53 end 1 Pet 3	Jer 31.23–40 Rom 12.1–8
Th	28	Isa 54 1 Pet 4	Jer 32.1–15 Rom 12.9–end
F	29	Isa 55 1 Pet 5	Jer 33.1–13 Rom 13
S	30	Isa 58.1–12 James 1.1–11	Jer 33.14–end Rom 14.1–12

O Lord, our King for ever, you listen to the prayers of the lowly, and hear the cries of the oppressed. Break the power of wickedness and evil, and fill your people with courage.

from Psalm 10

LENT 5

Be patient and tolerant towards one another, for the Lord himself is full of compassion and mercy.

from James 5

Day	Psalm	Year 1	Year 2
S		Jer 23.2–8 James 5.7–12	Deut 11.1–12 Luke 6.37–42
M	31	Isa 59.9–end James 1.12–end	Jer 37.1–10 Rom 14.13–end
T	32	Isa 60.1–12 James 2.1–13	Jer 37.11–21 Rom 15.1–13
W	33	Isa 60.13–end James 2.14–end	Jer 38.1–13 Rom 15.14–21
Th	34	Isa 61 James 3	Jer 38.14–end Rom 15.22–end
F	35	Isa 62 James 4	Jer 39.1–14 Rom 16.1–16
S	36	Isa 65.17–end James 5	Jer 42.1–12 Rom 16.17–end

O Lord, you are gracious and compassionate, slow to anger and quick to forgive. Give strength to your servants, and in your abiding love fill our hearts with gladness.

from Psalm 86

He emptied himself, taking the form of a servant; he humbled himself, and in obedience accepted even death.

from Philippians 2

Day	Psalm	Year 1	Year 2
S		Zech 9.9–12 Matt 21.1–13	Jer 7.1–7 Phil 2.6–11
M	5	Isa 8.16—9.1 Heb 2.5–end	Isa 8.16—9.1 Heb 2.5–end
T	17	Ezek 33.10–16 Rom 5.1–19	Ezek 33.10–16 Rom 5.1–19
W	29	Lev 16 Heb 9.11–14	Lev 16 Heb 9.11–14
Th	41	Exod 30.22–33 Matt 26.6–13	Judg 9.7–15 Mark 14.3–9
		MAUNDY THURSDAY COMMUNION Zech 13.7–end Matt 26.17–56	Isa 1.2–18 Mark 14.12–50
F	53	Isa 50.4–end Matt 26.57—27.26	Deut 21.1–9 Mark 14.53—15.15
		GOOD FRIDAY SERVICE Exod 26.31–35 Luke 23.26–49	Isa 52.13—53 end John 19.17–37
S	65	Job 14.1–14 Matt 27.57–end	Job 26.5–end John 19.38–end

O Lord God of truth, you see our distress and know our troubles, and you set our feet on the road to freedom. Into your hands we commit our spirits.

from Psalm 31

The Son of Man must be delivered into the hands of sinful men, and be crucified, and on the third day rise to life.

from Luke 24

Day	Psalm	Year 1	Year 2
S		EASTER DAY Isa 12 Luke 24.1–12	Isa 43.16–21 John 20.1–18
M	22	Exod 15.1–11 Matt 28	Exod 15.1–11 Matt 28
T	28	Sg of Sol 2.8–end Mark 16	Sg of Sol 2.8–end Mark 16
W	34	1 Kings 17.17–end John 21.1–14	1 Kings 17.17–end John 21.1–14
Th	40	Mic 7.7–end John 21.15–end	Mic 7.7–end John 21.15–end
F	46	Isa 25.1–5 Luke 24.13–35	Isa 25.1–5 Luke 24.13–35
S	52	Isa 42.10–16 Luke 24.36–45	Isa 42.10–16 Luke 24.36–45

Lord, you have turned our mourning into dancing; you have stripped off our sackcloth and clothed us in joy. May our hearts sing your praise and never be silent.

from Psalm 30

Confess your sins to one another and pray for one another, for the
prayers of righteous people have great power.

from James 5

Day	Psalm	Year 1	Year 2
S		Zech 8.1–13 Matt 5.21–26	Isa 59.9–end James 5.13–end
M	37	Amos 2.6–end Phil 1.1–11	Zeph 1.1–13 Col 1.1–14
T	38	Amos 3 Phil 1.12–26	Zeph 3.1–13 Col 1.15–23
W	39	Amos 4 Phil 1.27—2.11	Zeph 3.14–end Col 1.24—2.5
Th	40	Amos 5.1–9 Phil 2. 12–18	Hab 1.1–11 Col 2.6–19
F	41	Amos 5.10–17 Phil 2.19–end	Hab 1.12—2.4 Col 2.20—3.11
S	42	Amos 5.18–end Phil 3.1–11	Hab 2.5–11 Col 3.12—4.1

Father, may we know the peace of our Lord Jesus Christ,
who sacrificed himself for our sins to rescue us from all wickedness,
according to your will.

from Galatians 1

EASTER 2

Forgive one another, as the Lord has forgiven you.

from Colossians 3

Day	Psalm	Year 1	Year 2
S		Hos 14.4–8 Col 3.12–17	Num 14.11–22 John 8.1–11
M	43	Amos 6.1–7 Phil 3.12—4.1	Hab 2.12–end Col 4.2–end
T	44	Amos 6.8–end Phil 4.2–9	Hab 3 1 Tim 1.1–11
W	45	Amos 7.1–9 Phil 4.10–end	Hag 1 1 Tim 1.12–end
Th	46	Amos 8.4–end Rev 4	Hag 2.1–14 1 Tim 2
F	47	Amos 9.11–end Rev 5	Hag 2.15–end 1 Tim 3
S	48	Hos 1.1—2.1 Rev 6	Zech 1.1–17 1 Tim 4

O Lord, your presence fills us with joy. Reveal to us the wonders of your steadfast love, keep us as the apple of your eye, and protect us under the shadow of your wings.

from Psalm 17

EASTER 3

Your faith has made you whole; go in peace, and be healed.

from Mark 5

Day	Psalm	Year 1	Year 2
S		1 Kings 17.8–end Mark 5.21–end	2 Kings 5.1–14 Acts 3.1–10
M	49	Hos 2.2–13 Rev 7	Zech 1.18—2.5 1 Tim 5.1–16
T	50	Hos 2.14–end Rev 8	Zech 2.6–end 1 Tim 5.17—6.2
W	51	Hos 3 Rev 9.1–12	Zech 3 1 Tim 6.3–end
Th	52	Hos 4.1–10 Rev 9.13–end	Zech 4 1 Tim 7
F	53	Hos 4.11–end Rev 10	Zech 7 2 Tim 1.1–14
S	54	Hos 5 Rev 11.1–13	Zech 8.1–8 2 Tim 1.15—2.13

Lord, we live for you and you alone. Make us whole, turning our bitterness into peace, saving us from all danger and forgiving our sins.

from Isaiah 38

Divine folly is wiser than human wisdom, and divine weakness stronger than human strength.

from 1 Corinthians 1

Day	Psalm	Year 1	Year 2
S		Job 28.13–end 1 Cor 1.18–end	Jer 51.15–19 Matt 25.1–13
M	55	Hos 6.1—7.2 Rev 11.14–end	Zech 8.9–end 2 Tim 2.14–end
T	56	Hos 8 Rev 12	Zech 9.9–end 2 Tim 3.1–9
W	57	Hos 11.1–11 Rev 13.1–10	Zech 10.3–end 2 Tim 3.10—4.8
Th	58	Hos 11.12—12.6 Rev 13.11–end	Zech 11.4–end 2 Tim 4.9–end
F	59	Hos 12.7–end Rev 14.1–13	Zech 14.1–9, 20–end Titus 1
S	60	Hos 13 Rev 14.14–end	Mal 3.1–5 Titus 2

We pray that the God and Father of our Lord Jesus Christ
may give us the spirit of wisdom, that we may know fully the rich
blessings which he promises to all his people, and his immeasurable
power which is at work in all who believe.

from Ephesians 1

How great is the love in my heart for my people, and how deep my sympathy.

from Romans 9

Day	Psalm	Year 1	Year 2
S		Jer 29.4–14 Matt 5.43–end	Isa 63.7–17 Rom 9.1–5
M	61	Hos 14 Rev 15	Mal 3.6–12 Titus 3
T	62	Mic 1.1–7 Rev 16.1–11	Mal 4 Philemon
W	63	Mic 1.8–end Rev 16.12–end	Joel 1.1–12 Jude
Th	64	ASCENSION DAY 2 Kings 2.1–15 Luke 24.45–end	2 Kings 2.1–15 Luke 24.45–end
F	65	Mic 2 Rev 17	Joel 1.13–end Rev 1.1–8
S	66	Mic 3 Rev 18	Joel 2.1–17 Rev 1.9–end

O Lord, you are just in your works, and you are close to those who call upon you. May all mankind know your mighty acts, and look to you for every need.

from Psalm 145

EASTER 6

Welcome strangers into your homes, for some have thereby entertained angels without knowing it.

from Hebrews 13

Day	Psalm	Year 1	Year 2
S		Lev 25.35–38 Heb 13.1–8	Exod 22.21–27 Luke 16.19–end
M	67	Mic 4.1–7 Rev 19	Joel 2.18–27 Rev 2.1–7
T	68	Mic 4.8–end Rev 20	Joel 2.28–end Rev 2.8–11
W	69	Mic 5.2–end Rev 21.1–8	Jonah 1 Rev 2.12–17
Th	70	Mic 6.6–end Rev 21.9–21	Jonah 2 Rev 2.18–end
F	71	Mic 7.1–7 Rev 21.22—22.5	Jonah 3 Rev 3.1–13
S	72	Mic 7.14–end Rev 22.6–end	Jonah 4 Rev 3.14–end

Thanks be to God, who in Christ leads us in triumph, and who uses us to reveal and spread everywhere the sweet fragrance of the knowledge of himself.

from 2 Corinthians 2

PENTECOST WEEK

You shall receive power when the Holy Spirit has come upon you, and you shall be my witnesses.

from Acts 1

Day	Psalm	Year 1	Year 2
S		Gen 11.1–9 Acts 1.6–9; 2.1–11	Exod 19.16–end John 20.19–29
M	12	1 Kings 19.1–18 Acts 6.8–end	1 Kings 19.1–18 Acts 6.8–end
T	24	Ezek 37.1–14 Acts 7.54–end	Ezek 37.1–14 Acts 7.54–end
W	36	Isa 44.1–5 Acts 8.4–25	Isa 44.1–5 Acts 8.4–25
Th	48	Job 32.6b–end Gal 5.16–25	Job 32.6b–end Gal 5.16–25
F	60	Ezek 1.28b—2.5 1 Cor 3	Ezek 1.28b—2.5 1 Cor 3
S	72	Num 11.16–29 1 Cor 12.4–13	Num 11.16–29 1 Cor 12.4–13

Lord, you are our hope, reminding us constantly of your merciful kindness. Let your loving Spirit lead us, teaching us to do your will.

from Psalm 143

PENTECOST 1

The Son of Man did not come to be served, but to serve, and to give
his life as a ransom for many.

from Mark 10

Day	Psalm	Year 1	Year 2
S		1 Sam 10.1–7 Mark 10.35–45	Isa 45.1–6 Acts 3.11–end
M	1	Prov 1.1–19 Acts 1.1–14	Eccl 1 Luke 4.1–15
T	2	Prov 1.20–end Acts 1.15–end	Eccl 2.1–11 Luke 4.16–30
W	3	Prov 2 Acts 2.1–13	Eccl 2.12–end Luke 4.31–end
Th		INSTITUTION OF THE COMMUNION	
	4	Exod 12.1–14 Luke 22.14–20	Deut 16.1–8 1 Cor 11.23–29
F	5	Prov 3.1–12 Acts 2.14–36	Eccl 3.1–15 Luke 5.1–11
S	6	Prov 3.13–end Acts 2.37–end	Eccl 3.16–end Luke 5.12–26

May the God of grace who raised from the dead our Lord Jesus,
the great shepherd of the sheep, make us ready to do his will, turning
us into that which is pleasing in his sight.

from Hebrews 13

Feed yourselves on the words of faith and on true teaching, that you may be good servants of Christ.

from 1 Timothy 4

Day	Psalm	Year 1	Year 2
S		1 Sam 12.1–25 1 Tim 4.1–10	Isa 41.1–10 John 16.25–end
M	7	Prov 4 Acts 3.1–10	Eccl 4 Luke 5.27–end
T	8	Prov 6.1–19 Acts 3.11–end	Eccl 5 Luke 6.1–16
W	9	Prov 8.1–21 Acts 4.1–12	Eccl 6 Luke 6.17–36
Th	10	Prov 8.22–end Acts 4.13–22	Eccl 7.1–12 Luke 6.37–end
F	11	Prov 9 Acts 4.23–31	Eccl 8 Luke 7.1–17
S	12	Prov 10.1–13 Acts 4.32—5.11	Eccl 9.1–10 Luke 7.18–35

We thank you, Father, that through your Son Jesus Christ we are able to give strength to one another. We pray that our mutual encouragement in the faith may grow and deepen.

from Romans 1

This is how we can be sure of being in union with God: that we live as Christ lived, obeying his commandments.

from 1 John 2

Day	Psalm	Year 1	Year 2
S		Jer 32.6–15 Mark 7.24–30	Gen 28.10–end 1 John 2.3–11
M	13	Prov 14.31—15.17 Acts 5.12–26	Eccl 9.11–end Luke 7.36–end
T	14	Prov 22.1–16 Acts 5.27–end	Eccl 11.1–8 Luke 8.1–15
W	15	Prov 22.22–29 Acts 6.1–7	Eccl 11.9—12.8 Luke 8.16–25
Th	16	Prov 23.12–25 Acts 6.8–end	Eccl 12.9–end Luke 8.26–39
F	17	Prov 24.1–12 Acts 7.1–16	Esth 1 Luke 8.40–end
S	18	Prov 24.13–22 Acts 7.17–29	Esth 2.1–14 Luke 9.1–9

We thank you, Father, that you have chosen us as your own.
May we put our faith into action, working in a spirit of love in the service of our Lord Jesus Christ.

from 1 Thessalonians 1

Do not try to rule those who have been put in your care, but be examples to them. For God resists the proud, but favours the humble.

from 1 Peter 5

Day	Psalm	Year 1	Year 2
S		Josh 1.1–9 1 Pet 5.1–11	Josh 24.14–27 Luke 14.15–24
M	19	Prov 24.23–end Acts 7.30–38	Esth 2.15–end Luke 9.10–20
T	20	Prov 25.1–12 Acts 7.39–53	Esth 3.1–7 Luke 9.21–27
W	21	Prov 30.1–10 Acts 7.54–end	Esth 3.8–end Luke 9.28–36
Th	22	Prov 30.10–20 Acts 8.1–8	Esth 4 Luke 9.37–50
F	23	Prov 30.24–31 Acts 8.9–25	Esth 5 Luke 9.51–end
S	24	Prov 31.1–9 Acts 8.26–end	Esth 6 Luke 10.1–16

Let us pray that God may guide us to do what is right, in accordance with the truth, that we may grow in the perfect love of Christ Jesus our Lord.

from 2 Corinthians 13

PENTECOST 5

When the Spirit of truth comes, he will lead you in all truth.

from John 16

Day	Psalm	Year 1	Year 2
S		2 Sam 7.18–end John 15.26—16.15	Deut 30.11–end Rom 10.5–13
M	25	Prov 31.10–end Acts 9.1–19	Esth 7 Luke 10.17–24
T	26	Ezra 1 Acts 9.20–31	Job 1 Luke 10.25–37
W	27	Ezra 3 Acts 9.32–end	Job 2 Luke 10.38—11.13
Th	28	Ezra 4.1–5 Acts 10.1–16	Job 3 Luke 11.14–28
F	29	Ezra 4.6–end Acts 10.17–33	Job 4 Luke 11.29–36
S	30	Ezra 5 Acts 10.34–end	Job 5 Luke 11.37–end

Lord, you are all around us, and we cannot escape from your presence. Search us out, examining our hearts and discovering our thoughts, that you may guide us in the way of eternal life.

from Psalm 139

PENTECOST 6

Submit to one another out of reverence for Christ.

from Ephesians 5

Day	Psalm	Year 1	Year 2
S		Prov 4.1–9 Eph 5.15—6.4	Job 42.1–6 Mark 1.21–28
M	31	Ezra 6.1–12 Acts 11.1–18	Job 6 Luke 12.1–12
T	32	Ezra 6.13–end Acts 11.19–end	Job 7 Luke 12.13–21
W	33	Ezra 7.1–10 Acts 12.1–11	Job 8 Luke 12.22–34
Th	34	Ezra 7.11–end Acts 12.12–end	Job 9 Luke 12.35–48
F	35	Ezra 8.15–23 Acts 13.1–12	Job 10 Luke 12.49–end
S	36	Ezra 8.24–end Acts 13.13–25	Job 11 Luke 13.1–9

Protect us, O God, for we put our trust in you. We thank you that you guide our thoughts and instruct our hearts, showing us the path that leads to life.

from Psalm 16

PENTECOST 7

Be quick to listen, but slow to speak and slow to anger.

from James 1

Day	Psalm	Year 1	Year 2
S		Isa 51.4–8 Luke 10.38–end	Eccl 9.13–end James 1.19–end
M	37	Ezra 9 Acts 13.26–41	Job 12 Luke 13.10–21
T	38	Ezra 10.1–17 Acts 13.42–end	Job 13 Luke 13.22–end
W	39	Neh 1 Acts 14.1–7	Job 14 Luke 14.1–11
Th	40	Neh 2.1–10 Acts 14.8–20	Job 15.1–16 Luke 14.12–24
F	41	Neh 2.11–end Acts 14.21–end	Job 15.17–end Luke 14.25–end
S	42	Neh 4.1–9 Acts 15.1–11	Job 16 Luke 15.1–10

Father, we pray that you will fill us with all spiritual wisdom
and understanding, that our lives may bear fruit in every good work,
and that we may grow in knowledge of you.

from Colossians 1

God gives us insight into his will, that our lives may be worthy of him, bearing fruit in every good work.

from Colossians 1

Day	Psalm	Year 1	Year 2
S		Isa 61 Col 1.3–14	Isa 49.1–7 John 8.12–19
M	43	Neh 4.10–end Acts 15.12–21	Job 17 Luke 15.11–end
T	44	Neh 5.1–13 Acts 15.22–35	Job 18 Luke 16.1–18
W	45	Neh 5.14–end Acts 15.36—16.5	Job 19 Luke 16.19–end
Th	46	Neh 6.1–16 Acts 16.6–24	Job 20 Luke 17.1–10
F	47	Neh 8.1–12 Acts 16.25–end	Job 21 Luke 17.11–19
S	48	Neh 8.13–end Acts 17.1–15	Job 22 Luke 17.20–end

O Lord, you know the hearts of all your people. Show us the tasks that you want each person to perform in your service.

from Acts 1

You call me Lord and Master, and that is what I am. I have given you an example, that you also should do as I have done for you.

from John 13

Day	Psalm	Year 1	Year 2
S		Gen 18.1–5 John 13.2–17	Gen 32.22–30 Rev 19.5–16
M	49	Neh 9.1–5 Acts 17.16–end	Job 23 Luke 18.1–14
T	50	Neh 9.6–23 Acts 18.1–17	Job 24 Luke 18.15–30
W	51	Neh 9.24–end Acts 18.18–end	Job 25 & 26 Luke 18.31–end
Th	52	Neh 13.1–14 Acts 19.1–10	Job 27 Luke 19.1–10
F	53	Neh 13.15–end Acts 19.11–22	Job 28 Luke 19.11–27
S	54	Dan 1 Acts 19.23–end	Job 29 Luke 19.28–40

You, O Lord, are king for ever, and your name shall be known in every generation. Hear our prayers, and let our cry come unto you.

from Psalm 102

God has given us a ministry, to proclaim Jesus Christ as Lord, and to be servants of his people.

from 2 Corinthians 4

Day	Psalm	Year 1	Year 2
S		1 Kings 19.1–18 2 Cor 4.1 -6	Isa 58.1–12 Matt 6.1–13
M	55	Dan 2.1–13 Acts 20.1–16	Job 30 Luke 19.41—20.8
T	56	Dan 2.14–23 Acts 20.17–end	Job 31.1–23 Luke 20.9–26
W	57	Dan 2.24–35 Acts 21.1–16	Job 31.24–end Luke 20.27–40
Th	58	Dan 2.36–end Acts 21.17–26	Job 32 Luke 20.41—21.4
F	59	Dan 3.1–18 Acts 21.27–36	Job 33.1–30 Luke 21.5–19
S	60	Dan 3.19–end Acts 21.37—22.16	Job 38.1–21 Luke 21.20–end

We thank you, Father, that by the power of the Spirit you sanctify and teach us. May we stand firm and hold fast to your truth, doing and saying what is right, to the glory of your Son, Jesus Christ our Lord.

from Thessalonians 2

PENTECOST 11

Fulfil the ministry which has been entrusted to you in the Lord.

from Colossians 4

Day	Psalm	Year 1	Year 2
S		Ezek 34.11–16 John 10.1–16	Num 27.15–end Col 4.2–17
M	61	Dan 4.1–18 Acts 22.17–29	Job 38.22–end Luke 22.1–13
T	62	Dan 4.19–27 Acts 22.30—23.11	Job 39 Luke 22.14–23
W	63	Dan 4.28–end Acts 23.12–end	Job 40 Luke 22.24–34
Th	64	Dan 5.1–12 Acts 24.1–23	Job 41 Luke 22.35–46
F	65	Dan 5.13–end Acts 24.24—25.12	Job 42 Luke 22.47–62
S	66	Dan 6.1–10 Acts 25.13–end	Sg of Sol 1.1—2.7 Luke 22.63—23.5

Lord, you have shown your great and steadfast love throughout
all generations. Give us the wisdom to exercise authority with justice
and to discern the difference between good and evil.

from Kings 3

PENTECOST 12

May your hearts be knit together in love, that you may come to understand the mystery of God's love.

from Colossians 2

Day	Psalm	Year 1	Year 2
S		Isa 28.23–end Col 2.1–10	1 Kings 12.1–17 John 3.1–21
M	67	Dan 6.11–end Acts 26.1–18	Sg of Sol 2.8—3.5 Luke 23.6–25
T	68	Dan 7.1–14 Acts 26.19–end	Sg of Sol 3.6—5.1 Luke 23.26–43
W	69	Dan 7.15–end Acts 27.1–26	Sg of Sol 5.2—6.3 Luke 23.44–end
Th	70	Dan 9.1–19 Acts 27.27–end	Sg of Sol 6.4–end Luke 24.1–12
F	71	Dan 9.20–end Acts 28.1–16	Sg of Sol 7.1—8.4 Luke 24.13–35
S	72	Dan 12 Acts 28.17–end	Sg of Sol 8.5–end Luke 24.36–end

Give us, Lord, the desire to obey your commandments, and teach us their meaning, that we may follow them throughout our lives, and receive the joy which you promise to all who love you.

from Psalm 119

FESTIVAL PSALMS AND READINGS

(in addition to those already included)

Date	Psalm	Year 1	Year 2
January 1st	33	THE NAMING OF CHRIST Isa 9.2–7 Luke 2.15–21	Gen 17.1–14 Luke 2.15–21
January 6th	58	THE EPIPHANY OF CHRIST Isa 49.1–6 Matt 2.1–12	Isa 42.1–7 Matt 3.13–end
January 25th	21	THE CONVERSION OF ST PAUL Isa 6.1–8 Acts 9.1–22	Jer 1.4–10 Gal 1.11–end
February 2nd	16	THE PRESENTATION OF CHRIST Exod 13.11–16 Luke 2.22–38	Jer 23.1–6 Luke 2.22–38
March 25th	70	THE ANNUNCIATION OF CHRIST Mic 5.2–4 Luke 1.26–38	Isa 7.10–15 Luke 1.26–38
June 24th	51	THE BIRTH OF JOHN THE BAPTIST Mal 3.1–5 Luke 1.57–66, 80	Isa 40.1–11 Luke 3.1–9
June 29th	27	THE PASTORAL MINISTRY (FEAST OF ST PETER) Job 29.11–17 1 Pet 5.1–4	Eccl 12.9–end Matt 16.13–20
August 6th	10	THE TRANSFIGURATION OF CHRIST Exod 34.29–end Matt 17.1–13	Isa 60.1–9 Luke 9.28–36
September 29th	15	ST MICHAEL AND ALL ANGELS Dan 6.11–23 Matt 18.1–6, 10	1 Chron 21.1–17, 27–28 Rev 12.7–12

October 18th		THE HEALING MINISTRY (FEAST OF ST LUKE)	
	9	1 Kings 18.41–end	2 Kings 4.38–end
		Luke 11.14–22	Luke 7.1–17

November 1st		ALL SAINTS	
	69	Jer 31.31–34	Mal 2.5–7
		Heb 12.18–24	Rev 7.2–4, 9–end

November 30th		THE MISSION OF THE CHURCH (FEAST OF ST ANDREW)	
	39	Isa 52.7–10	Isa 61.1–3
		Luke 10.1–9	Matt 10.5–15

December 4th		CHRISTIAN COMMUNITY (FEAST OF NICHOLAS FERRAR)	
	57	Exod 19.1–6	Gen 45.1–15
		John 17.20–end	Acts 2.38–end

December 26th		THE MARTYRS OF THE CHURCH (FEAST OF ST STEPHEN)	
	63	2 Chron 24.17–22	Jer 11.18–20
		Acts 7.54–end	Acts 26.1–18

December 28th		THE HOLY INNOCENTS	
	45	Jer 31.15–17	Isa 65.17–end
		Matt 2.13–18	Mark 10.13–16

PSALMS

These are for use during Daily Prayer. The number to be used each day is given in the calendar of sentences, readings and collects.

1 THE FULNESS OF GOD

1 The desert will rejoice and flowers will bloom in the wilderness:
the desert will sing and shout for joy.
2 Everyone will see the splendour of the Lord: his greatness and
power.
3 Give strength to hands that are weak, make firm knees that
tremble: take courage and be strong, for God is coming to your
rescue.
4 The eyes of the blind shall be opened: the ears of the deaf
unstopped.
5 The lame will leap and dance: the dumb shall sing for joy.
6 Water shall flow through the desert: the burning sand shall
become a lake.
7 And a highway shall be there: it shall be called the Road of
Holiness.
8 No lions will be there: no fierce animals will pass that way.
9 Those whom the Lord has redeemed shall travel home by it:
they shall rejoice and sing.
10 They shall be free from sorrow and grief: eternal joy shall be
upon them.

from Isaiah 35

1 Christ is the image of the invisible God: he is the first-born of all
creation.
2 In him all things were created in heaven and on earth: all things
were created through him and for him.
3 He existed before all things: in him are all things held together.
4 He is the head of the body: he is the source of the body's life.
5 He is the first-born from the dead: he alone has first place in all
things.
6 In him the fulness of God is present: through him all things are
reconciled.
7 Through the blood of his cross God made peace: he brought the
whole universe back to himself.

from Colossians 1

2 THE ARMOUR OF GOD

1 The Lord has seen the falsehood of the wicked: that truth stumbles in the public square, and honesty cannot enter.
2 He is displeased that no one helps the oppressed: that justice is driven away, and righteousness stands far off.
3 So his own arm shall rescue the oppressed: he shall win victory.
4 He will put on armour as a breastplate: and the helmet of salvation on his head.
5 He will clothe himself with fury: with desire to set right the wrongs which people suffer.
6 In the west they will fear his name: in the east they will tremble at his glory.
7 He will appear like a rushing river: like a strong wind he will come upon his people.
8 His spirit will fill them with power: and his word will guide their steps for all generations.

from Isaiah 59

1 Put on the armour of God: be strong in the Lord.
2 We are not fighting against flesh and blood, but against cosmic forces: against the principalities and powers of this dark age.
3 So put on God's armour now: resist the enemy's attack, and stand firm to the end.
4 Let truth be your belt, and righteousness your breastplate: as shoes wear readiness to preach the gospel of peace.
5 Carry faith as your shield: with it you can quench the flaming arrows of the evil one.
6 Let salvation be your helmet: as a sword take the word of God.
7 Pray at all times in the Spirit: keep alert at all times and never surrender.

from Ephesians 6

3 GOOD AND EVIL

1 Today I give you the choice between good and evil: between life and death.
2 The Lord your God is one Lord: love the Lord your God with all your heart, with all your soul, and with all your strength.
3 Let these words be on your heart: teach them to your children when you are at home or away, resting or working.
4 Obey the commandments of God: follow the path of the Lord.
5 Do not put the Lord your God to the test: do what is right and good, and all shall go well with you.
6 For the Lord is faithful and he will keep his covenant: his love will be constant for a thousand generations to those who love him.

from Deuteronomy 6, 7, 11 and 30

1 God, for whom and by whom all things exist, made his Son Jesus Christ perfect through suffering: to lead many sons to salvation.
2 He purifies people from their sins: so that he is not ashamed to call them brothers.
3 He became like us, sharing our human nature: that he might destroy the devil, who has power over death.
4 He became like us in every way: to be our faithful and merciful High Priest in the service of God.
5 He is able to help those who are tempted: because he himself suffered and was tempted.
6 So our sins are forgiven: we are set free from our slavery.

from Hebrews 2

4   THE BREAD OF LIFE

1   I love the Lord because he hears my voice: he listens to my prayers.
2   The Lord is gracious and righteous: he is full of compassion.
3   What can I offer the Lord: how can I repay his goodness?
4   I will lift up the cup of salvation: and call upon the name of the Lord.
5   Lord, I am your servant: you have freed me from my bonds.
6   I will offer you a sacrifice of thanksgiving: I will call upon the name of the Lord.

from Psalm 116

1   I am the living bread which comes down from heaven: whoever eats this bread will live for ever.
2   I am the bread of life: the bread which I give for the life of the world is my flesh.
3   He who comes to me will never be hungry: he who believes in me will never be thirsty.
4   He who comes to me I will not turn away: but I will raise him to life.
5   Whoever eats my flesh and drinks my blood abides in me: and I abide in him.
6   As the living Father sent me: so he who eats me will live because of me.

from John 6

5 DYING AND LIVING IN CHRIST

1 Is there any sorrow like my sorrow: which the Lord has inflicted on me in his burning anger?

2 He sent fire from above, fire that burnt within me: then he left me deserted, stunned and faint all day long.

3 His hand bound my sins into a yoke: he hung them round my neck, and I grew weak beneath their weight.

4 My eyes flow with tears: no one can comfort me or give me courage.

5 I stretch out my hands, but no one will help me: the Lord has summoned enemies against me on every side.

6 But the Lord is just: for I have rebelled against his word.

7 Look, Lord, at my agony, the anguish of my soul: my heart is broken in sorrow for my sins.

from Lamentations 1

1 We were buried with Christ in baptism: and in baptism we were raised with him.

2 We were dead in spirit: but God has brought us to life in Christ.

3 He forgave our sins: he nailed to the cross the bonds which enslaved us.

4 We have died with Christ on the cross: he set us free from the elemental spirits.

5 We have been raised to life with Christ: when Christ appears we also shall appear with him in glory.

from Colossians 2

6 THE BODY OF CHRIST

1 Sing to the Lord, all the earth: serve the Lord with gladness.
2 Come into his presence with songs of joy: know that the Lord is our God.
3 It is he who made us and we are his: we are his people and the sheep of his pasture.
4 Come into his gates with thanksgiving: and into his courts with praise.
5 Give thanks to him: and bless his holy name.
6 For the Lord is good, his love is everlasting: his faithfulness endures throughout all generations.

from Psalm 100

1 There is one body and one spirit: one hope to which God has called us.
2 There is one Lord, one faith, one baptism: one God and Father, who works through all, and is in all.
3 There are many parts in the one body: we are joined to each other as different parts of one body.
4 Each one of us has received a special gift: let us use it according to God's grace.
5 If it is to speak God's message, speak it in faith: if it is to teach, serve, or encourage others, do so with devotion.
6 So we shall come together in unity of faith and knowledge: we shall grow up in every way to Christ, who is the Lord.
7 Under him all the different parts of the body fit together: the whole body grows and builds itself up in love.

from Romans 12 and Ephesians 4

7 THE KINGDOM OF HEAVEN

1 A king shall reign in righteousness: leaders shall govern with justice.
2 Each will be like a shelter from the wind: a place to hide from storms.
3 They will be like streams of water in the desert: like the shade of a great rock in a barren land.
4 Their eyes will be open to the needs of the people: their ears will hear them.
5 They will no longer be impatient: but they will act with understanding and will speak with honesty.
6 God will pour out his Spirit: the desert will become fertile, and the fields will yield rich crops.
7 Justice will dwell in the land: righteousness will be everywhere.
8 And righteousness will bring peace and trust: God's people will be secure and safe in their homes.

from Isaiah 32

1 The kingdom of heaven is like a mustard seed: the smallest of all seeds.
2 When it is grown up it is the greatest of all plants: birds come and rest in its branches.
3 The kingdom of heaven is like treasure hidden in a field: the man who finds it sells all he has to buy that field.
4 It is like a merchant in search of fine pearls: he finds one pearl of great value, and sells all he has to buy it.
5 The kingdom of heaven is like yeast: a woman mixes it with flour until the whole dough rises.
6 It is like a net thrown into the sea: when it is full the men draw it ashore, putting the good fish into vessels and throwing the bad away.

from Matthew 13

8   THE WORD MADE FLESH

1 God is our shelter and strength: ready to help in time of trouble.
2 We will not fear though the earth is shaken: though the mountains tumble into the sea.
3 Though the seas roar and rage: though the mountains quake at the rising of the sea.
4 There is a river whose streams make glad the city of God: the holy dwelling place of the Most High.
5 God is in the midst of her and she shall not be destroyed: God will help her at the break of day.
6 The Lord Almighty is with us: the God of Jacob is our refuge.
7 Come and see the works of the Lord: what he has done on earth.
8 He makes wars to cease in all the world: he breaks the bows, shatters the spears, and burns the chariots.
9 Be still and know that I am God: exalted among the nations, exalted upon the earth.
10 The Lord Almighty is with us: the God of Jacob is our refuge.

from Psalm 46

1 The Word became flesh: he dwelt among us, full of grace and truth.
2 We saw his glory: glory which he received as the only Son of the Father.
3 From his fulness we have all received: grace upon grace.
4 The law was given through Moses: grace and truth came through Jesus Christ.
5 No one has ever seen God: the only Son, who is nearest to the Father's heart, has made him known.

from John 1

9 GOD'S MIGHTY ACTS

1 You have rejected us, O God, and broken us: now turn back to us.
2 You have made the earth tremble and torn it apart: now heal its
   wounds.
3 You have allowed your people to suffer: to drink a bitter wine
   that makes us stagger.
4 But you have warned those who fear you: so they can escape
   condemnation.
5 Save us by your power: answer our prayer, and rescue those who
   are dear to you.
6 Help us in this hour of crisis: the help that man can give is
   worthless.

from Psalm 60

1 'Lord, if it is your will: you can make me clean.'
2 'I do will it: be clean.'
3 'Lord, I am not worthy to receive you: only say the word and I
   shall be healed.'
4 'Truly, I have never found anyone in Israel with faith like this: go,
   and what you believe will be done.'
5 'If I only touch the Lord's cloak: I shall be made whole.'
6 'Courage, my daughter: your faith has made you whole.'
7 'Son of David, have mercy on us: we believe you can make us see.'
8 'Then it shall be done to you according to your faith: receive your
   sight.'

from Matthew 8 and 9

1   How lovely is your dwelling place: O Lord of hosts.

2   My soul longs for the courts of the Lord: my heart and my flesh
    rejoice in the living God.

3   The sparrow has found a home and the swallow a nest for her
    young: your altars, my king and my God.

4   Blessed are those who dwell in your house: they will always sing
    your praises.

5   Blessed are those whose strength is in you: who, going through
    the valley of dryness, find a spring from which to drink.

6   One day in your courts is better than a thousand elsewhere: I
    would rather stand at the door of the house of my God than dwell
    in the tents of ungodliness.

7   For the Lord is a rampart and a shield, giving grace and glory: he
    withholds nothing from those who walk in innocence.

8   O Lord of hosts: blessed is the man who puts his trust in you.

from Psalm 84

1   Out of the darkness light shines: we see the glory of God.

2   His glory shines in the face of Christ: for Christ is the very image
    of God.

3   This same glory transforms us also: God's light shines in our
    hearts, that we too reflect his glory.

4   We put aside all secret and shameful deeds: we do not act with
    deceit, nor falsify God's word.

5   In the full light of truth we live in God's sight: by this we
    commend ourselves to the consciences of others.

6   So may God's grace reach more and more people: that they may
    swell the chorus of thanksgiving to the glory of God.

from 2 Corinthians 3 and 4

11 COME AND REST

1 O God, put a curse on the day of my birth: on the night when I was conceived.

2 Let gloom and darkness descend on that day: let no joy be heard in that night.

3 I wish I had died in my mother's womb: or died at the moment of birth.

4 I would be at rest now: sleeping like a still-born child.

5 Why give life to those who live in misery: why give light to men bitter in soul?

6 They long for death, but it never comes: they prefer the grave to any treasure.

7 Everything I fear comes true: I have no peace, no rest.

8 But I know that my redeemer lives: and at last he will stand upon the earth.

9 I shall see him with my own eyes: and he will not be a stranger.

from Job 3 and 19

1 I thank you, Father, that you have revealed to the unlearned what is hidden from the wise and learned: such was your choice.

2 No one knows the Son except the Father: and no one knows the Father except the Son, and those to whom the Son reveals him.

3 Come to me, all whose work is hard, whose load is heavy: and I will give you rest.

4 Take my yoke upon you and learn from me: for I am gentle and humble of heart.

5 My yoke is easy: my burden is light.

from Matthew 11 and Luke 10

12 THE COMING OF THE SPIRIT

1 Blow the trumpet in Zion: sound the alarm on the holy mountain.
2 Let the people of Judah tremble: the day of the Lord is near.
3 Gather the people together: prepare them for a sacred meeting.
4 Assemble the elders and the children: even the nursing infants.
5 Let the bridegroom leave his room: and the bride her chamber.
6 The priests, the ministers of the law: they must weep and pray.
7 I will pour out my spirit on all people: your sons and daughters shall proclaim my message.
8 Your old men shall dream dreams: and your young men shall see visions.
9 I will give signs that day in heaven and on earth: there will be bloodshed, fire and columns of smoke.
10 The sun will be turned to darkness: the moon will be turned to blood.
11 All who call upon the name of the Lord: will be saved.

from Joel 2

1 God has raised Christ from death: and exalted him to his right hand.
2 Christ has received from the Father the promise of the Holy Spirit: and this gift he has poured upon us.
3 The Holy Spirit has come: and we are filled with his power.
4 So we shall be Christ's witnesses in Jerusalem, Judea and Samaria: and to the ends of the earth.
5 May all who hear attend: and be baptized in the name of Jesus Christ.
6 Their sins will be forgiven: and they shall receive the gift of the Holy Spirit.

from Acts 1 and 2

13 HOLY, HOLY, HOLY

1 Give thanks to the Lord, proclaim his greatness: make known his deeds among the nations.
2 The Lord is our God: his commands are for all the world.
3 He will keep his covenant for ever: his promises for a thousand generations.
4 Sing to the Lord and bless his holy name: proclaim the good news of his salvation.
5 Glory and majesty surround him: power and beauty fill his temple.
6 Worship the Lord in the beauty of his holiness: tremble before him all the earth.
7 Let the heavens be glad and the earth rejoice: let the sea roar and all that fills it.
8 Let the fields rejoice and all that is in them: the trees in the woods shout for joy.
9 For he comes to rule the earth: he shall rule the world with justice, and the peoples with his truth.

from 1 Chronicles 16

1 Holy, holy, holy is the Lord God Almighty: who was and is and is to come.
2 Glory and honour and power: are yours by right, O Lord our God.
3 For you created all things: and by your will they have their being.
4 Glory and honour and power: are yours by right, O Lamb that was slain.
5 For by your blood you ransomed men for God: from every race and tongue, from every people and nation.
6 To make them a kingdom of priests: to stand and serve before our God.
7 To him who sits on the throne and to the Lamb: be praise and honour, glory and might, for ever and ever.

from Revelation 4

14 LIGHT TO THE WORLD

1 Listen to me, distant nations: hear my words, you who live in far-off lands.
2 The Lord chose me before I was born: he called me to be his servant.
3 He made my words as sharp as a sword: he formed me like a sharpened arrow.
4 He appointed me to bring back his people: to gather his scattered children.
5 In the eyes of the Lord I am honoured: God is my strength.
6 The Lord says: 'I will make you a light to the nations: that all the world may be saved.
7 Kings will arise when they see you: princes will bow before you.'
8 This will happen because the Lord is faithful: the holy God of Israel has chosen his servant.

from Isaiah 49

1 Lord, now let your servant depart in peace: your word has been fulfilled.
2 My own eyes have seen your salvation: which you have prepared in the presence of all peoples.
3 A light to reveal you to the Gentiles: and bring glory to your people Israel.

from Luke 2

15 GOD'S PURPOSE

1 I will restore my people and have compassion on every family: I
   will heal their wounds and make them well.
2 My people will sing a song of thanksgiving: they will shout for
   joy.
3 I will bless them and they will multiply: my blessing shall bring
   them honour.
4 Their prince shall be one of themselves: their rulers shall come
   from their midst.
5 I shall call him: and he will draw near me.
6 Their communities shall be established firmly in my presence:
   they shall be my people, and I shall be their God.

from Jeremiah 30

1 Blessed be the God and Father of our Lord Jesus Christ: in Christ
   he has given us every spiritual blessing in the heavenly world.
2 God chose us in Christ before the world was made: that we should
   be holy and blameless before him.
3 We praise God for his glorious grace: for the free gift he has given
   us in his dear Son.
4 By the death of Christ we are set free, our sins are forgiven:
   through him God has made us his sons.
5 God has revealed his purpose in Christ: to unite all creation,
   everything in heaven and on earth, with Christ as head.
6 All things are done according to God's purpose: he has chosen us
   to be his people, to praise his glory.
7 He has sealed us with his Holy Spirit: which is the promise of
   freedom for all his people.
8 How rich are the blessings he promises to his people: how great is
   his power at work within us.

from Ephesians 1

1   The Lord is my light and my salvation: I shall fear no one.
2   The Lord is the strong castle of my life: I shall never be afraid.
3   One thing I have asked from the Lord which I require: to dwell in
    the house of the Lord all the days of my life;
4   To look upon the beauty of the Lord: and to seek his will.
5   In times of trouble he will shelter me: he will hide me in his tent,
    he will lift me high upon the rocks.
6   With shouts of joy I will offer sacrifices in his sanctuary: I will
    sing and praise the Lord.
7   Teach me your way, O Lord: lead me on an easy path.
8   I shall surely see the goodness of the Lord: in the land of the living.
9   Stand firm and he will put courage in your heart: trust in the
    Lord.

from Psalm 27

1   God is light: in him there is no darkness at all.
2   If we claim to be sharing his life while we walk in darkness: we lie
    in word and action.
3   If we walk in light as he himself is in the light: then we share
    together in a common life, and we are purified from every sin.
4   The darkness is passing away: the true light already shines.
5   Whoever hates his brother is in darkness: he is blind and cannot
    see his path.
6   Whoever loves his brother lives in the light: there is nothing to
    make him stumble.

from 1 John 1 and 2

17 SORROW AND JOY

1 Remember, Lord, what has happened to us: look at us and see our disgrace.

2 Joy has vanished from our hearts: our dancing has been turned to mourning.

3 Nothing is left of our proud achievements: we have sinned and we are doomed.

4 Our hearts are sick: our eyes are dim with tears.

5 But you, Lord, reign for ever: your throne endures from age to age.

6 Why have you abandoned us for so long: will you ever remember us again?

7 Restore us to yourself, Lord, and we will return: renew our ancient glory.

8 Or have you rejected us for ever: is there no limit to your anger?

from Lamentations 5

1 In a little while you will see me no more: and then a little while later you will see me.

2 You will cry and weep, but the world will rejoice: you will be sorrowful, but your sorrow will be turned into joy.

3 A woman in labour is in pain because her hour has come: but when the baby is born she forgets the anguish, for joy in the birth of her child.

4 So it is with you, that now are sad at heart: but I will see you again and you will rejoice.

5 On that day the Father will give you anything you ask for in my name: ask and receive, that your joy may be complete.

6 For the Father himself loves you: he loves you because you love me and believe that I came from him.

7 Take courage, for the victory is mine: I have conquered the world.

from John 16

1   They will listen and listen, but not understand: they will look and look, but not see.
2   Their hearts are dull: they have stopped up their ears, and closed their eyes.
3   Otherwise their eyes would see and their ears hear: their hearts would understand.
4   They would turn to me: and they would be healed.
5   It will be like this until their cities are ruined: and their houses empty.
6   I will send them to a far-off land: and make their land a desolate waste.
7   The people who remain will be like the stump of an oak tree that has been felled: they will make a new beginning.

from Isaiah 6

1   Blessed are you: to you it has been given to know the secrets of the kingdom of heaven.
2   Blessed are your eyes and your ears: your eyes see and your ears hear.
3   Many prophets and righteous men longed to see what you see: to hear what you hear.
4   The Father has revealed to the unlearned what is hidden from the wise and learned: such was his choice.
5   He has revealed that I am his Son: he has given the knowledge directly to you.
6   So be perfect: as your Father in heaven is perfect.

from Matthew 13, 16 and 5

19 THE ATHLETES OF GOD

1 Teach me, O Lord, the way of your statutes: I will follow it to the end.
2 Give me understanding, that I may obey your laws: I will obey them with all my heart.
3 Give me the desire to follow your commands: rather than to seek riches.
4 Guide me in the way of your precepts: in them I find happiness.
5 Guide me away from vanities: give me life as I walk in your way.
6 Show me how much you love me: save me according to your promise.
7 Show me how to speak the truth: my hope is in your judgements.
8 I shall live in perfect freedom: because I seek to obey your laws.
9 I shall live in perfect happiness: because I love your laws.

from Psalm 119

1 We strive to win the prize which Christ has won for us: we forget what is behind and reach our for what lies ahead.
2 We do not claim to have succeeded: we are not already perfect.
3 But we press on towards the goal: to win God's call through Christ to eternal life.
4 Every athlete submits to strict discipline, to be crowned with a perishable wreath: we do it for an imperishable wreath.
5 We rid ourselves of everything that impedes us: of the sin which clings so closely.
6 We run straight for the finishing line: our eyes fixed on Jesus.

from Philippians 3, 1 Corinthians 9 and Hebrews 12

20   THE QUALITIES OF LOVE

1   Praise the Lord, O my soul: let all that is within me praise his holy name.
2   He forgives all my sins: and heals all my diseases.
3   He redeems my life: and crowns me with love and mercy.
4   He gives justice to the oppressed: and works for righteousness.
5   He is full of compassion and mercy: slow to anger and constant in love.
6   He does not punish us as we deserve: nor repay us for our sins.
7   As the sky is high above the earth: so great is his love for those who follow him.
8   As a father is tender to his children: so the Lord is tender to those who honour him.
9   Praise the Lord, you strong and mighty angels: who listen to his word and obey his commands.
10   Praise the Lord, you heavenly powers: his servants who do his will.
11   Praise the Lord, all his creatures under his rule: praise the Lord, O my soul.

from Psalm 103

1   Love is patient and kind: it is not jealous or boastful, not arrogant or rude.
2   Love does not insist on its own way: it is not irritable or resentful.
3   Love does not rejoice at wrong: it rejoices in the right.
4   Love bears all things, believes all things: it hopes all things, endures all things.
5   Prophecies, tongues and knowledge will cease: for they are imperfect.
6   Love never ends: for love is perfect, and when the perfect comes the imperfect will pass away.
7   Now we see in a mirror dimly: but then we shall see face to face.
8   Now I know in part: but then I shall understand fully, even as I have been fully understood.
9   So faith, hope, love abide, these three: but the greatest of these is love.

from 1 Corinthians 13

21 GOOD NEWS

1 The Spirit of the Lord God is upon me: the Lord has chosen me,
2 To bring the good news to the poor and heal the broken-hearted: to proclaim liberty to those in prison.
3 He has sent me to announce that the time has come: when the Lord will save his people.
4 He has sent me to comfort those who mourn: to give a garland instead of ashes, the mantle of praise instead of a faint spirit.
5 They will be called oaks of righteousness: trees that the Lord himself has planted to glorify him.
6 His people will be called priests of the Lord: the ministers of our God.
7 They will be famous among the nations: all who see them will know that they are blessed by the Lord.

from Isaiah 61

1 Go to my lost sheep and preach: 'The kingdom of heaven is at hand.'
2 Heal the sick and raise the dead: cleanse lepers and cast out demons.
3 You have received freely: so freely give.
4 Take no gold, silver nor copper, no extra shirts or sandals: the worker should earn his keep.
5 When you enter a house, bless it: if the house is worthy, let your peace come upon it.
6 If anyone will not receive you or listen to you: shake the dust from your feet as you leave that place.
7 I am sending you out as sheep among wolves: be wise as serpents and gentle as doves.
8 Do not be anxious about how you speak or what you say: it is not you who will speak, but the Spirit will be speaking through you.

from Matthew 10

22 NEW BIRTH

1 Our city is strong: God himself defends us.

2 Open the gates, let the faithful nation enter: the nation whose people are righteous.

3 The Lord gives peace to those whose minds are steadfast: who put their trust in him.

4 He has humbled the proud, bringing to the ground their lofty city: the feet of the poor and the lowly trample its dust.

5 Lord, you straighten the path of the upright: the road they travel is smooth.

6 At night my soul longs for you: my spirit yearns for you.

7 For when you judge the earth and its people: all will learn your justice.

8 Your people who have died will live again: their bodies will rise.

9 They will awake and sing for joy: as the sparkling dew refreshes the earth, so the Lord will give new life to the dead.

from Isaiah 26

1 Jesus has died and has risen: he will come again.

2 The Lord himself will descend from heaven: there will be a shout of command, and the sound of God's trumpet.

3 Those who have died in Christ will rise first: then we who are alive shall be gathered up with them.

4 The day of the Lord will come like a thief in the night: as suddenly as the pangs of a woman in labour.

5 But we are not in darkness: we shall not be taken by surprise.

6 We are children of light: we shall be alert and sober.

7 We shall always be with Christ: we shall live together with him.

from 1 Thessalonians 4 and 5

1 I have sent my people among the nations: I have scattered them in far-off countries.
2 Yet I am present with them: I have been a sanctuary for them in the lands where they have gone.
3 I will gather them together: and they shall know my holiness.
4 I will sprinkle clean water upon them: and purify them from all that has defiled them.
5 I will give them a single heart: and put a new spirit within them.
6 I will take away their stubborn hearts of stone: and give them obedient hearts of flesh.
7 They shall keep my laws and obey my commandments: they shall be my people, and I will be their God.

from Ezekiel 36

1 The kingdom of God is at hand: repent and believe in the gospel.
2 Come and follow me: I will make you fishers of men.
3 Foxes have holes and birds have nests: but the Son of Man has nowhere to lay his head.
4 I have chosen you to be with me: I will send you out to preach and to cast out demons.
5 Those who are well do not need a doctor: but only those who are sick.
6 I have not come to call the righteous and respectable: but the sinners and outcasts.
7 If anyone wants to come with me: he must forget self and take up his cross.
8 For whoever wants to save his own life will lose it: and whoever loses his life for my sake will find it.

from Matthew 8 and 16, and Mark 1, 2 and 3

24 BORN IN THE SPIRIT

1 I will cause breath to enter you: and you shall live.
2 I will raise you to life: and you shall know that I am the Lord.
3 I will put my Spirit within you: and you shall hear my word.
4 I will place you in your own land: and you will know that I the
  Lord have spoken.
5 I will save you from all your sins: and you shall be my people.
6 I will live among you: and you shall lift your heads high among
  the nations.

from Ezekiel 37

1 No one can enter the kingdom of God unless he is born anew:
  unless he is born of water and the Spirit.
2 That which is born of the flesh is flesh: that which is born of the
  Spirit is spirit.
3 The wind blows where it wills, and you hear its sound: but you
  do not know where it comes from or where it goes.
4 It is like that with everyone born of the Spirit: it is the Spirit that
  gives life.
5 The time is coming when people will worship the Father in truth:
  they will offer the worship he seeks.
6 God is Spirit: only by the power of the Spirit may he be
  worshipped in truth.

from John 3 and 4

25 THE WORD OF GOD

1 I am with them and am better than jewels: nothing you can desire can compare with me.
2 I speak the truth: lies are hateful to me.
3 I walk in the way of righteousness: I follow the path of justice.
4 The Lord created me at the beginning of his work: the first of his acts, long ago.
5 I was made in the very beginning: before the world began.
6 I was born before the oceans: when there were no springs of water.
7 I was born before the mountains had been formed: before God made the earth and its fields.
8 I was there when he set the sky in place: when he stretched the horizon across the ocean.
9 I was beside him like an architect: I was his daily delight, rejoicing always in his presence.
10 I rejoiced in the world: I delighted in the human race.
11 He who finds me finds life: and the Lord shall be pleased with him.

from Proverbs 8

1 In the beginning was the Word: the Word was with God and the Word was God.
2 All things were made through him: not one thing in all creation was made without him.
3 In him was life: this life brought light to mankind.
4 The light shines in the darkness: the darkness has never overcome it.
5 The Word was in the world, and the world was made through him: but the world did not know him.
6 He came to his own home: but his people did not receive him.
7 But to all who received him and believed in him: he gave the power to become the children of God.

from John 1

26 UNITY IN THE LORD

1 How good and lovely it is: when God's people live together in unity.
2 It is as fragrant as precious oil upon the head of Aaron: running down his head and beard to the collar of his robes.
3 It is like dew upon Mount Hermon: running down the hills of Zion.
4 For there the Lord has commanded his blessing: which is life for evermore.
5 Come and bless the Lord, all you his servants: you that by night serve in his temple.
6 Lift up your hands in the holy place: and bless the Lord.
7 May the Lord who made heaven and earth: bless you from Mount Zion.

from Psalms 133 and 134

1 Father, I pray that all who believe in me may be one: just as you and I are one.
2 I pray that they may be in us: just as you are in me and I in you.
3 The glory that you have given me I have given to them: that they may become perfectly one.
4 Thus shall the world know that you sent me: that you love them as you love me.
5 Father, I desire that those whom you have given me may be with me: that they may see my glory, the glory that you gave me.
6 The world does not know you, but I know you: and they know that you sent me.
7 I made your name known to them: that the love you have for me may be in them.

from John 17

27 THE GOOD SHEPHERD

1 I, the sovereign Lord, will search for my sheep: I will seek them out.
2 As a shepherd gathers his flock when they are scattered: so I will look after my sheep.
3 I will rescue them from the places where they have been scattered: I will bring them back to their own land.
4 I will lead them back to the rich pasture: they shall graze safely among mountains and valleys.
5 I will be the shepherd of my sheep: and find them a resting place.
6 I will look for those that are lost: and will bring back those that wander.
7 I will bandage those that are hurt: and heal those that are sick.
8 You, the flock that I feed, are my people: and I am your God.

from Ezekiel 34

1 I am the gate for the sheep: whoever enters by me shall be saved.
2 All who have come before me are thieves and robbers: but the sheep did not listen to them.
3 I came that you may have life: and have it abundantly.
4 I am the good shepherd: I am willing to die for my sheep.
5 The hired man leaves the sheep when he sees the wolf coming: he cares nothing for his sheep.
6 As the Father knows me and I know the Father: so I know my sheep and they know me.
7 I have other sheep not of this fold: I must bring them also.
8 They will heed my voice: they will be one flock with one shepherd.

from John 10

1   Lord, you are everlasting: you are my God, holy and eternal.
2   Your eyes are too holy to look upon evil: you cannot bear the sight of wrong-doing.
3   I have heard all you have done: I am filled with awe.
4   Now do again in our time: your great deeds of old.
5   May your glory cover the heavens: and the earth be full of your praise.
6   May the earth be filled with the knowledge of the glory of the Lord: as the waters cover the sea.

from Habakkuk 1, 2 and 3

1   Father, glorify your Son: that the Son may glorify you.
2   You gave me power over all mankind: that I might give eternal life to all whom you gave me.
3   And this is eternal life: to know you the only true God, and to know me whom you sent.
4   I have shown your glory on earth: the glory I shared with you before the world was made.
5   I have made your name known to the men you gave me from the world: they were yours, and you gave them to me.
6   They have obeyed your word: they know that everything you gave me comes from you.
7   I taught them all that I learned from you: they have received it, and they believe that I came from you.
8   All that I have is yours, and all that you have is mine: my glory is shown through them.

from John 17

1 I have suffered under the rod of God's anger: he drove me into the deepest darkness.

2 He has beaten me, leaving my flesh open and raw, and my bones broken: he has forced me into a prison of anguish, to dwell in the darkness of death.

3 He has bound me in chains: I cry for help, but he refuses to listen.

4 He rubbed my face in the ground and broke my teeth on the gravel: my strength is gone.

5 Yet hope returns when I remember his constant love: every morning his mercy is renewed, so great is his faithfulness.

6 I will put my hope in God: the Lord is good to those who wait for him, to the soul that seeks him.

7 The Lord is merciful, and will not reject us for ever: though he brings us grief, his love is sure and strong.

8 Let us examine our ways and return to the Lord: let us open our hearts to God and pray for his forgiveness.

from Lamentations 3

1 God has shown how much he loves us: that while we were still sinners Christ died for us.

2 We have been put right with God through faith: we have peace with God through our Lord Jesus Christ.

3 We have been baptized into Christ's death: by baptism we were buried with him.

4 So as Christ was raised from the dead by the glory of the Father: we too might walk in newness of life.

5 Since we have become one with him in dying: so we shall be one with him by being raised to life.

6 Our old self has been crucified with Christ: that our sinful self may be destroyed, and we may be freed from sin.

7 We have died with Christ: we shall live with him.

from Romans 5 and 6

1   I wanted to accept you, Israel, as my son: to give as a heritage the most beautiful land in the world.
2   I wanted you to call me Father: that you should never again turn away from me.
3   But as an unfaithful wife left her husband: so you have been unfaithful to me.
4   Return, faithless Israel, I will not look on you in anger: I am merciful and I shall not be angry for ever.
5   Return, faithless children, you belong to me: I will bring you back to Mount Zion.
6   I will give you shepherds after my own heart: they will fill you with wisdom and understanding.

from Jeremiah 3

1   If we have died with him: we shall also live with him.
2   If we endure: we shall also reign with him.
3   If we deny him: he also will deny us.
4   If we are faithless: he remains faithful, for he cannot be false to himself.
5   He saved us and called us his own people: not by our efforts but by his own purpose and grace.
6   He has ended the power of death: he has revealed through the gospel immortal life.

from 2 Timothy 1 and 2

1 Behold I am coming with fire: I will ride on the wings of a storm.
2 I am coming to gather all nations and tongues: and they shall see my glory.
3 By fire and sword I will punish the guilty: but some I will send to distant lands which have not seen my power.
4 To Spain and to Libya, to Tubal and Greece I will send them: they shall proclaim my greatness among the nations.
5 I am making a new earth and new heavens: I will give a new name to my servants.
6 Be glad and rejoice at what I create: no weeping shall be heard, no cries of distress.
7 Babies will no longer die in infancy: all people will live their full span.
8 Like trees my people will live long lives: I will bless my people, and answer their prayers.
9 The wolf and the lamb shall feed together: the lion shall eat straw like an ox, and dust shall be the serpent's food.
10 The new earth and the new heavens shall be upheld by my power: that people of every nation will worship me.

from Isaiah 65 and 66

1 By the word of God the heavens and earth were created: by the same word they are being preserved until the day of judgement.
2 With the Lord one day is as a thousand years: and a thousand years like one day.
3 The Lord is patient with us: he wants no one to be destroyed, but all to reach repentance.
4 The day of the Lord will come like a thief: the heavens will be burned and the earth will vanish.
5 On that day he will fulfil his purpose: he will create new heavens and a new earth, where righteousness shall dwell.
6 May we grow in the grace and knowledge of our Lord and Saviour Jesus Christ: to him be glory for evermore.

from 2 Peter 3

1   The people who walked in darkness have seen a great light: the light has shone upon those who lived in a land of deep shadow.
2   You have given them great joy: they rejoice at what you have done.
3   For you have broken the yoke that burdened them: you have snapped the rod that beat them.
4   You have defeated those who oppressed them: the boots and the blood-stained clothing of battle are destroyed by fire.
5   To us a child is born, to us a son is given: he will be our ruler.
6   He will be called Wonderful Counsellor, Mighty God: Eternal Father, Prince of Peace.
7   His kingdom will always live in peace: he will rule with justice and integrity to the end of time.

from Isaiah 9

1   Hail Mary, full of grace: the Lord is with you.
2   Blessed are you among women: and blessed is the fruit of your womb.
3   Behold you shall conceive in your womb and bear a son: you shall give him the name Jesus.
4   He will be great, and will be called the Son of the Most High: and the Lord God will give to him the throne of his father David.
5   He will reign over the house of Jacob for ever: and his kingdom will have no end.
6   The Holy Spirit will come upon you: the power of the Most High will overshadow you.
7   The child to be born will be called holy: he will be the Son of God.

from Luke 1

1   Praise the Lord, praise the Lord from the heavens: praise him in the heights above.
2   Praise him, sun and moon: praise him all shining stars.
3   Let them praise the name of the Lord: for he commanded and they were created.
4   Praise the Lord from the earth: praise him, you sea monsters and all the ocean depths.
5   Praise him, lightning and hail, mist and snow: strong winds that obey his command.
6   Praise him, hills and mountains, fruit trees and forests: all wild beasts and cattle, all creeping things and birds.
7   Praise him, kings of the earth and all people: princes and rulers of the world.
8   Praise him, young men and maidens: old and young together.
9   Let them praise the name of the Lord: his name alone is exalted.
10 His glory is above heaven and earth: let all his children praise him.

from Psalm 148

1   How great is our Father's love: he has called us his children.
2   We are now the children of God: when Christ appears we shall be like him.
3   Everyone who has this hope purifies himself: as Christ himself is pure.
4   The child of God does not sin, for God's nature is within him: God is his Father and he cannot sin.
5   The child of God loves God and keeps his commandments: for his commands are never too hard.
6   The child of God defeats the world: for he who believes that Jesus is the Son of God wins victory by means of his faith.

from 1 John 3 and 5

1 In the days to come the mountain of the temple of God will be the highest of all mountains: it shall be raised above the hills.

2 All the nations shall stream to it: people without number shall come to it.

3 So let us go up to the mountain of God: to the house of the God of Jacob.

4 He shall teach us his ways: that we may walk in the paths he has chosen.

5 He shall settle disputes among the nations: and wield authority near and far.

6 And they shall hammer their swords into ploughs: their spears into pruning knives.

7 Nation shall not lift sword against nation: never again shall they study the art of war.

8 Everyone shall live in peace among his own vineyards and trees, and no one shall be afraid: the Lord of Hosts has spoken.

from Micah 4

1 If anyone is in Christ, he is a new creation: the old has passed away, the new has come.

2 Christ has reconciled us with God: God was in Christ, reconciling the world to himself, forgiving all people their sins.

3 God has given us the task of reconciling others: he has entrusted us with his gospel of reconciliation in Christ.

4 We are ambassadors for Christ, God making his appeal through us: we plead on Christ's behalf.

5 Christ was without sin, but for our sake he shared our sin: that in union with him we might share the righteousness of God.

6 We are ruled by the love of Christ: we live not for ourselves but for him who died and rose.

From 2 Corinthians 5

1   I waited patiently for the Lord: he listened to me and heard my cry.

2   He drew me up out of the pit of groaning, out of mud and dirt: he set my foot upon a rock, and made firm my foothold.

3   He put a new song on my lips: a song of thanksgiving to our God.

4   O Lord, my God, how great are your thoughts and actions for us: there is none to be compared with you.

5   You do not desire sacrifices and offerings: instead you have given me ears to hear you.

6   Here I am, O God: I long to do your will.

7   I proclaim the good news of your salvation among the people: I cannot restrain myself.

8   I speak always of your faithfulness: your loyalty and constant love.

9   Your mercies, O Lord, will never cease: your love and truth will always keep me safe.

from Psalm 40

1   Christ has appeared once and for all: he has put away sin by the sacrifice of himself.

2   Christ was offered once to bear the sins of many: he will appear a second time to save those who are waiting for him.

3   Christ obeyed the will of God by his sacrifice: so we are purified from sin.

4   We are set free to enter the sanctuary: he has opened for us a living way into God's presence.

5   Let us draw near to God in faith, with hearts purified from guilt: for God's promises are sure.

6   Let us encourage one another: for the day of the Lord draws near.

from Hebrews 9 and 10

1 Lord, your steadfast love reaches the heavens: your faithfulness extends to the skies.
2 Your righteousness is like the high mountains: your justice is like the depths of the sea.
3 How precious, O God, is your enduring love: we take refuge under the shadow of your wings.
4 We feast on the good food of your house: we drink from the river of your goodness.
5 You are the fountain of all life: in your light we shall see light.
6 Continue your steadfast love to those who know you: your justice to those who are true of heart.

from Psalm 36

1 God who raised Jesus from the dead will give life to our mortal bodies: for his Spirit dwells within us.
2 All who are led by the Spirit of God are sons of God: the Spirit makes us God's children.
3 By the Spirit's power we cry out to God, 'Abba', Father: the Spirit himself bears witness with our spirits that we are children of God.
4 The Spirit helps us in our weakness: for we do not know how to pray as we ought.
5 The Spirit intercedes for us with sighs too deep for words: and God, who searches the hearts of men, knows the mind of the Spirit.
6 We are fellow-heirs with Christ of God's blessings: if we share Christ's suffering, we shall share also his glory.

from Romans 8

1   Lord, there is none like you: you are mighty and your name is
    great and powerful.
2   Among all the sages and kings of the world: there is none like you.
3   You are the true and living God, the eternal King: at your anger
    the world trembles.
4   You made the earth by your power: by your wisdom you created
    the world and stretched out the heavens.
5   At your command the waters above the sky roar: you bring
    clouds from the ends of the earth.
6   You make the lightning flash in the rain: you bring forth wind
    from your storehouses.
7   Lord, no one is master of his own destiny: no man can direct his
    own life.
8   Do not be angry with us, for that would destroy us: but correct us,
    Lord, with justice.

from Jeremiah 10

1   Great and wonderful are your deeds, Lord God the Almighty: just
    and true are your ways, King of the nations.
2   Who will not fear you and praise your name, O Lord: for you
    alone are holy?
3   All nations will come and worship in your presence: for your just
    actions have been revealed.
4   Praise our God, all you his servants: all people, both great and
    small, worship him.
5   Let us rejoice and be glad, let us praise his glory: for the marriage
    of the Lamb has come.
6   His bride has made herself ready: with fine pure linen, the good
    deeds of God's people.
7   Blessed are those who are invited to the marriage supper of the
    Lamb: come, gather for the great supper of God.

from Revelation 15 and 19

1   Praise the Lord, praise the Lord, O my soul: all my life I will sing
praises to my God.
2   Put not your trust in princes: no human being can save you.
3   For when their breath goes from them they return to the dust:
on that day all their plans perish.
4   Blessed is the man whose help is the God of Jacob: whose hope is
in the Lord his God.
5   The God who made heaven and earth: the sea, and all that is in
them.
6   He keeps faith for ever: he deals justly with those who are
oppressed.
7   The Lord gives food to the hungry: and sets the captives free.
8   He gives sight to the blind: he lifts up those who have fallen.
9   The Lord loves the righteous: he cares for the stranger in the
land.
10   He upholds the widow and the orphan: but the plans of the
wicked he brings to ruin.
11   The Lord is king for ever: your God, O Zion, shall reign through
all generations.

from Psalm 146

1   No man can serve two masters: you cannot serve both God and
mammon.
2   Do not be anxious about food and clothes: life is more than food,
and the body is more than clothes.
3   Look at the birds of the air: they neither sow nor reap nor gather
into barns.
4   Yet your Father in heaven feeds them: are you not worth much
more than the birds?
5   Consider the lilies of the field: they neither toil nor spin.
6   Yet your Father in heaven clothes them: even Solomon in all his
glory was not arrayed like one of these.
7   Seek first the kingdom of God and his justice: and all you need
shall be yours as well.

from Matthew 6

1 Awake and be strong: clothe yourself with splendour.
2 Shake yourself from the dust and arise: loose the chains which bind you and be free.
3 How beautiful upon the mountains is the messenger who brings the good news: who proclaims that God is king.
4 He brings news of peace: he announces salvation to God's people.
5 Break into songs of joy: see with your own eyes the coming of the Lord.
6 The Lord will rescue his people: he will protect and comfort them.
7 The Lord will go before them and behind them: he will save his people and the world shall see it.
8 The Lord says, 'My people shall know my name: on that day they shall know it is I who speak.'

from Isaiah 52

1 All authority in heaven and on earth has been given to me: you are my witnesses.
2 Go then to all peoples everywhere: make them my disciples.
3 Baptize them in the name of the Father, the Son and the Holy Spirit: teach them to observe all my commandments.
4 He who believes and is baptized will be saved: he who does not believe will be condemned.
5 Believers will cast out demons in my name: they will lay hands on the sick, who will get well.
6 And lo, I am with you always: to the end of the age.

from Matthew 28, Mark 16 and Luke 24

1   I seek the help of the Lord and he answers me: he frees me from all my sins.
2   The poor man cries and the Lord hears him: he saves him from all his troubles.
3   The angel of the Lord guards those who obey him: he rescues them from danger.
4   Taste and see that the Lord is good: happy is the man who finds safety in him.
5   Lions go hungry for lack of food: but those who seek the Lord lack nothing.
6   The Lord is near the broken hearted: he saves those who are crushed in spirit.
7   The righteous man suffers many trials: but the Lord rescues him from them all.
8   The Lord takes care of him: not one of his bones is broken.
9   The Lord redeems the lives of his servants: all those who take shelter in him have nothing to pay.

from Psalm 34

1   Christ suffered for us, leaving us his example: we are to follow his steps.
2   He committed no sin: no lie was heard from his lips.
3   When he was insulted he did not give insults in return: when he suffered he did not threaten.
4   He bore our sins on his body on the cross: that we might die to sin and live to righteousness.
5   By his wounds we have been healed: by his death he leads us to God.
6   Through him we put our trust in God, who raised him from death and gave him glory: in him our hope is fixed on God.

from 1 Peter 1, 2 and 3

1 He has borne our suffering and carried our sorrow: yet we thought his suffering was punishment sent by God.

2 He was wounded for our faults: he was beaten for our sins.

3 We are healed by the punishment he suffered: made whole by the blows he received.

4 We had gone astray like lost sheep: each had taken his own way.

5 But the Lord laid upon him our sins: he took the burden which we deserved.

6 He was treated harshly but bore it humbly: he never opened his mouth.

7 Like a lamb led to the slaughter, like a sheep before its shearers: he never opened his mouth.

8 He was arrested, sentenced, and led off to die: no one pleaded his cause.

9 They put him in a grave with the wicked: he was buried with the rich.

10 He was put to death for the sins of our people: though he had committed no crime and spoken no lie.

from Isaiah 53

1 In the world rulers lord it over their subjects: they have complete authority.

2 But it shall not be so with you: whoever wants to be great must be the servant of all.

3 The highest among you must become as the youngest: the leader must become like the slave.

4 The Son of Man comes to you not to be served: but to serve and give his life as a ransom for many.

5 Everyone who has left houses or brothers or sisters or children or lands for my sake: will receive eternal life.

6 Many who are now first will be last: and many who are now last shall be first.

from Matthew 19 and 20, and Luke 22

42 ASK, SEEK, KNOCK

1 You, Lord, are my refuge and defence: guide me and lead me as you have promised.
2 Into your hands I commit my spirit: you redeem me, Lord God of truth.
3 I will rejoice and be glad in your loving kindness: you see my suffering, you know my distress.
4 In you I put my trust: you are my God.
5 Make your face shine upon your servant: and save me in your constant love.
6 How plentiful is your goodness, stored up for those who honour you: how securely you protect those who put their trust in you.
7 Blessed be the Lord our God: how wonderfully he showed his love when I was as a city besieged.
8 I was afraid and thought he had driven me from his presence: but he heard my cry when I called for help.
9 Love the Lord, all his faithful people: the Lord God guards the true but requites the proud.
10 Be strong, and let your heart take courage: all you that hope in the Lord.

from Psalm 31

1 Ask and you will receive: everyone who asks receives.
2 Seek and you will find: he who seeks finds.
3 Knock and it will be opened to you: to him who knocks the door is opened.
4 Would you give your son a stone when he asks for bread: would you give him a snake when he asks for fish?
5 You know how to give good things to your children: how much more will your Father in heaven give to those who ask.
6 If two of you agree when you pray: it will be done for you by your Father in heaven.
7 Where two or three gather in my name: I am there in the midst of them.

from Matthew 7 and 18

43 STRENGTH IN GOD

1 Hear me, O God, and answer me: for I am helpless and weak.
2 I call to you in times of trouble: for you hear my prayers.
3 Show me your way, O Lord, and I will walk in your truth: teach me to serve you with devotion.
4 I will praise you, O Lord my God, with all my heart: I will proclaim your glory for ever.
5 How great is your abiding love towards me: you have saved me from the lowest depths of the grave.
6 You are compassionate and gracious: slow to anger, loving and faithful.
7 Turn to me in your mercy, O Lord, and give me strength: you are my helper and comforter.

from Psalm 86

1 Love one another with all your strength: for love covers a multitude of sins.
2 Be good stewards of God's grace: for each has received a special gift.
3 Whoever preaches should preach God's word: whoever serves should serve with all his might.
4 Be sober, be watchful: your adversary the devil prowls about like a roaring lion, seeking someone to devour.
5 Resist him, firm in the faith: remember that your brother Christians throughout the world share your sufferings.
6 The God of grace calls you to his eternal glory in Christ: he will restore and strengthen you on a firm foundation.
7 To him be power for ever: to those who live in him be peace.

from 1 Peter 4 and 5

1 I will make you my wife: I will be true and faithful.
2 I will show you love and mercy: and you shall know me as your Lord.
3 I will make a covenant for you with the beasts and the birds: that they shall not harm you.
4 I will abolish all weapons of war, all swords and bows: that you may live in peace and safety.
5 I will make rain fall on the earth: that it may give corn and grapes and olives.
6 I will show love to those who are unloved: I will proclaim as my people those who are not my people.

from Hosea 2

1 Let us love one another, for love is of God: he who loves is born of God and knows God.
2 In this the love of God was made manifest among us: that God sent his only Son into the world, that we might live through him.
3 This is love: not that we love God, but that he loved us and sent his Son to be the expiation for our sins.
4 If God so loves us, we ought also to love one another: if we love one another, God abides in us and his love is perfected in us.
5 There is no fear in love: but perfect love casts out fear.
6 We love because God first loved us: he who abides in love abides in God, and God abides in him.

from 1 John 4

1 When Israel was a child I loved him: out of Egypt I called my son.

2 It was I who taught Israel to walk: I took him in my arms.

3 I drew him to me with cords of love, holding him to my cheek: I bent down to him and led him.

4 How can I give you up, O Israel: how can I abandon you?

5 My heart recoils from punishing you: my love is too warm and tender.

6 I will heal your faithlessness: I will love you with all my heart.

7 I will be to you like rain in the desert: you shall blossom like a flower.

8 Your beauty shall be like the olive tree, your fragrance like the wine of Lebanon: your shoots shall spread out, and your roots shall be strong.

9 I will answer your prayers and look after you: I am the source of all your happiness.

from Hosea 11 and 14

1 Let the children come to me and do not hinder them: the kingdom of heaven belongs to such as these.

2 Do not despise any little ones: their angels in heaven are always in the presence of the Father.

3 Unless you turn and become like children: you will never enter the kingdom of heaven.

4 Whoever humbles himself like a child: he is the greatest in the kingdom of heaven.

5 Whoever welcomes a child in my name: welcomes me.

from Matthew 18 and 19

1 Let the heavens praise your wonders, O Lord: let them sing of your faithfulness.
2 I know your love will last for ever: your faithfulness is as permanent as the sky.
3 Who is like you, Lord God of hosts: your power and faithfulness are all about you.
4 You rule the raging of the sea: when its waves rise, you still them.
5 The heavens are yours, and so is the earth: you made the world and all that is in it.
6 Your kingdom is founded on righteousness and justice: love and faithfulness are shown in all you do.
7 Happy are those who worship you with songs: who live in the light of your kindness.
8 You are their glory and strength: our heads are lifted up by your love.

from Psalm 89

1 Jesus Christ, Lamb of God: you take away the sin of the world.
2 You love us and have freed us from our sins by your blood: you are the first-born of the dead, the ruler of the kings on earth.
3 We thank you that you have taken your great power: that your reign has already begun.
4 You will come upon the clouds: everyone will see you, even those who pierced you.
5 You are the first and the last: to you be glory and power for evermore.

from John 1 and Revelation 1 and 11

1 Blessed is the man whose sin is forgiven: whose wrongs are pardoned.
2 Blessed is the man whom God does not accuse: and in whose spirit there is no deceit.
3 When I did not confess my sins: my bones wasted away from crying all day long.
4 Your hand was heavy upon me day and night: my strength was drained like moisture dried up in the summer heat.
5 When I acknowledged my sins to you: I did not hide my wrongdoings.
6 I decided to confess to you: and your forgave my wickedness.
7 So all your faithful people should pray to you in times of trouble: when a great flood of trouble comes rushing in it will not reach them.
8 You are my hiding place, you save me from trouble: I sing aloud of your salvation.
9 You teach us the way we should go: those who put their trust in you are embraced by your constant love.

from Psalm 32

1 Do not judge others: and you will not be judged.
2 Do not condemn others: and you will not be condemned.
3 Why do you see the speck in your brother's eye: but ignore the log in your own eye?
4 First take the log from your own eye: then you will see clearly to take the speck out of your brother's eye.
5 Forgive others: and you will be forgiven.
6 Give to others: and it will be given to you.
7 A full measure, pressed down and running over: will be poured into your lap.

from Matthew 7 and Luke 6

48   THE SPIRIT OF TRUTH

1 Have mercy on me, O God, in your steadfast love: in your compassion blot out all my sins.
2 You require sincerity and truth: fill my heart with your wisdom.
3 Remove my sin, and I shall be clean: wash me and I shall be whiter than snow.
4 Fill me with joy and gladness: let the bones which you have broken rejoice.
5 Create in me a pure heart, O God: renew a right spirit within me.
6 Do not banish me from your presence: do not take your Holy Spirit from me.
7 Revive in me the joy of your salvation: grant me a steady and willing spirit.
8 Then I will teach your ways to sinners: and they shall return to you again.
9 O Lord, open my lips: and my mouth shall proclaim your praise.
10 You take no pleasure in sacrifice, or I would give it: you do not want burnt offerings.
11 My sacrifice, O God, is a broken spirit: you will not reject a humble and contrite heart.

from Psalm 51

1 I shall pray to the Father and he will send you a Counsellor: the Spirit who will be with you for ever.
2 The world cannot receive him because it cannot see or know him: you know him, for he dwells within you.
3 The Spirit whom the Father will send in my name: will bear witness to me.
4 He will confute the people of the world: showing where right and wrong and judgement lie.
5 He will guide you in all truth: and he will glorify me.
6 He will not speak on his own authority: but he will speak what he hears, and will tell of things to come.
7 All that the Father has is mine: and the Spirit will take what is mine and declare it to you.

from John 14 and 16

1 I will gather my people from the farthest corners of the earth: the blind and the lame, and the woman with child, shall return.

2 With weeping they shall come: they shall be praying as I lead them back.

3 I will guide them by streams of water: on a smooth road where they will not stumble.

4 So stop your weeping: wipe away your tears.

5 The days are coming when I will make a new covenant with my people: not like the old covenant I made with their fathers which they broke.

6 I will put my law within them: I will write it upon their hearts.

7 I will be their God: and they shall be my people.

8 All shall know me: from the least to the greatest.

9 I will forgive their sins: I will remember their wrongs no more.

from Jeremiah 31

1 The word of God is alive and active: it is sharper than any two-edged sword.

2 It pierces to where soul and spirit meet, to where joint and marrow come together: it discerns the thoughts and intentions of the heart.

3 Nothing can be hid from God: every creature is exposed and laid bare before his eyes.

4 Let us keep our eyes fixed on Jesus: he is the pioneer and perfecter of our faith.

5 Because of the joy that was waiting for him, he despised the shame of the cross: he is seated at the right hand of the throne of God.

6 He endured from sinners such hostility against himself: that you may not grow weary or fainthearted, but reap the peaceful fruits of a righteous life.

7 Lift up your tired hands, and strengthen your trembling knees: strive for peace with everyone and live a holy life.

8 You have come to the city of the living God: you have come to Jesus, the mediator of the new covenant.

from Hebrews 4 and 12

50 PREPARING FOR CHRIST

1 Prepare the way of the Lord: make straight his path in the wilderness.
2 Fill every valley and level every mountain: the hills shall become a plain, and rough land made smooth.
3 The glory of the Lord shall be revealed and all mankind shall see it: the Lord himself has spoken.
4 All men are like grass, and their beauty is like that of wild flowers: the grass withers and the flowers fade when the breath of the Lord blows upon them.
5 People last no longer than grass: but the word of the Lord endures for ever.
6 Climb up the high mountain and proclaim the good news: cry out with courage that the Lord is coming.
7 The Lord is coming to rule with power: he will bring with him the people he has rescued.
8 He will feed his flock like a shepherd: and gather the lambs in his arms.

from Isaiah 40

1 Turn from your sins and be baptized: God will forgive you.
2 The axe is laid at the roots of the trees: every tree that does not bear good fruit will be cut down and thrown in the fire.
3 Whoever has two coats must give one to the man who has none: whoever has food must share it with the man who is hungry.
4 Be content with what you have: do not use violence or deceit.
5 Amongst you stands one you do not know: he is the one on whom the Spirit rests.
6 He is the Chosen One of God: he will baptize with the Holy Spirit and with fire.

from Luke 3 and John 1

51   THE PROMISE OF CHRIST

1   The day is coming, glowing like a furnace: when the proud and the arrogant will be like stubble.

2   That day shall burn them up: it will leave neither root nor branch.

3   But for you who obey me my saving power shall rise upon you like the sun: there shall be healing in its rays.

4   You shall leap like calves from the stall: you shall trample the wicked like dust under your feet.

5   But before that great and terrible day: I will send my prophet.

6   He will turn the hearts of fathers to their children: and the hearts of children to their fathers.

from Malachi 4

1   Blessed be the Lord, the God of Israel: for he has come to his people and set them free.

2   He raised up for us a mighty saviour: born of the house of his servant David.

3   Through his holy prophets he promised long ago: that he would save us from our enemies, from the hands of all that hate us.

4   He promised to show mercy to our fathers: and to remember his holy covenant.

5   This is the oath that he swore to our father Abraham: to set us free from the hands of our enemies.

6   Free to worship him without fear: that we might be holy and righteous in his sight all the days of our life.

7   You my child will be called the prophet of the Most High: for you will go before the Lord to prepare his way.

8   To tell the people that they will be saved: by the forgiveness of all their sins.

9   In the compassion of our Lord: the dawn of salvation will rise upon us.

10   To shine from heaven on all who live in the shadow of death: and to guide out steps in the way of peace.

from Luke 1

1 Turn to me and be saved, all the ends of the earth: for I am God and there is no other.

2 My promise is true: and it shall not be changed.

3 To me every knee shall bow: every tongue vow loyalty.

4 They will say that in me alone is victory and strength: all who hate me will be disgraced.

5 I am your God and shall support you: I made you, and shall care for you.

6 Confess that I alone am God: there is none like me.

7 Listen to me, faint hearts: those that feel victory is far away.

8 I bring victory near, already it is close: my salvation shall not be delayed.

from Isaiah 45 and 46

1 Let not your hearts be troubled: trust in God and trust also in me.

2 My Father's house has many rooms: I am going to prepare a place for you.

3 I will return and take you to myself, that where I am you will be also: you know the way where I am going.

4 I am the way, the truth and the life: no one comes to the Father but by me.

5 If you knew me, you would know my Father also: from now on you do know him and have seen him.

6 He who has seen me has seen the Father: I am in the Father and the Father is in me.

7 He who believes in me will do the work that I do: and greater works than these he will do, because I go to the Father.

8 Whatever you ask in my name shall be done, that the Father may be glorified in the Son: if you ask anything in my name, I will do it.

from John 14

53 THE PASSION OF CHRIST

1 My God, my God, why have you forsaken me: I have cried in desperation for help, but still it does not come.
2 My God, I call to you by day but you do not answer: I call at night but get no rest.
3 All who see me laugh me to scorn: they stick out their tongues and shake their heads, saying,
4 'You trusted in the Lord, let him save you: let him rescue you if he delights in you.'
5 Lord, in you have I trusted since my birth: you have always been my God.
6 Do not leave me now trouble is near: there is no one to help.
7 My strength is gone like water spilt on the ground: my bones are out of joint, and my heart is like melted wax.
8 My throat is as dry as dust: my tongue clings to the roof of my mouth.
9 All my bones can be seen: my enemies look at me and stare.
10 They divide my garments among themselves: they cast lots for my clothing.
11 O Lord, do not stand far off: come quickly to my rescue.

from Psalm 22

1 As Pilate tried him, Jesus said: 'My kingdom is not of this world;
2 I came into this world to bear witness to the truth: everyone who belongs to the truth hears my voice.'
3 As the soldiers nailed him to the cross, Jesus said: 'Father, forgive them, they know not what they do.'
4 As the criminal beside him asked for his blessing, Jesus said: 'Today you shall be with me in paradise.'
5 As he was hanging on the cross, Jesus said: 'It is finished.'
6 As he died, Jesus said: 'Father, into your hands I commit my spirit.'

from John 18 and 19 and Luke 23

54   THE PEOPLE OF GOD

1   O Lord, you were gracious to your land: you restored the fortunes of Jacob.

2   You forgave your people's sins: and pardoned them all their wrongs.

3   You put aside your anger: and held back your furious rage.

4   Let me hear what the Lord will say: he will speak to his people, his saints whose hearts are turned to him.

5   Surely his salvation is near to those who honour him: that his glory may dwell in our land.

6   Love and faithfulness will meet: justice and peace will kiss.

7   Truth will spring from the earth: and righteousness will look down from heaven.

8   The Lord will give what is good: and our land will yield its plenty.

9   Righteousness will go before the Lord: and prepare the path for him.

from Psalm 85

1   You are the people of God: he loved you and chose you for his own.

2   Be tolerant with each other: forgive one another as the Lord has forgiven you.

3   Clothe yourselves with compassion and kindness, gentleness and patience: to these add love, which binds all together in perfect harmony.

4   Let the peace of Christ guide your decisions: for it is to this peace that God has called you together.

5   Let the word of Christ in all its richness dwell in your hearts: teach one another with all wisdom.

6   Sing psalms and hymns and spiritual songs: sing to the Lord with thankful hearts.

7   Do everything in the name of the Lord Jesus: Christ is all and is in all.

from Colossians 3

55 WISDOM AND FOLLY

1 Those who are wise come to worship me: but their words are meaningless.
2 Their hearts are far from me: their religion is nothing but traditions and rules learned by rote.
3 So I will startle them: I will act as they do not expect.
4 The wisdom of the wise will perish: their cleverness will be useless.
5 Foolish men shall understand: those who grumble will receive instructions gladly.
6 The ears of the deaf will hear the words of books: the eyes of the blind will see light.
7 The meek will receive new joy: the poor will rejoice in the Lord.
8 My people, you shall no longer be disgraced: your faces shall never again pale with shame.

from Isaiah 29

1 The gospel of Christ on the cross is folly to those who are being lost: but to those who are being saved it is the power of God.
2 God in his wisdom made it impossible for the world to know him through wisdom: God saves those who believe in the folly of the gospel.
3 Jews demand miracles, Greeks seek wisdom: but our gospel is Christ crucified, offensive to Jews and nonsense to Gentiles.
4 Yet the folly of God is wiser than the wisdom of men: the weakness of God is stronger than the strength of men.
5 When God called us few were wise by wordly standards: not many were powerful or of noble birth.
6 Buy God chose what is foolish to shame the wise: he chose what is weak to shame the strong.
7 God chose what is low and despised in the world: to destroy what the world thinks is important.
8 God has made Christ our wisdom: by him we become God's people and are set free.

from 1 Corinthians 1

1   Holy, holy, holy is the Lord of Hosts: his glory fills the whole
     world.
2   There is no hope for me, I am lost: yet my own eyes have seen the
     King, the Lord of Hosts.
3   I have heard him say, 'Whom shall I send, who will be our
     messenger?': and I answered, 'Here I am, take me.'
4   Hear then house of David: the Lord himself will give you a sign.
5   A young woman will conceive and bear a son: and will call him
     Emmanuel.
6   When he is old enough to refuse the evil and choose the good:
     people will be drinking milk and eating honey.

from Isaiah 6 and 7

1   Glory to God in the highest: on earth peace and goodwill among
     men.
2   Behold, I bring you good news: great joy to all people.
3   In the city of David your saviour is born: Christ the Lord.
4   This will be a sign: a babe lying in a manger wrapped in
     swaddling clothes.
5   Glory to God in the highest: on earth peace and goodwill among
     men.

from Luke 2

57 THE LIVING STONE

1 Open to me the gates of righteousness: that I may enter and give thanks to the Lord.
2 This is the gate of the Lord: the righteous shall come in.
3 I praise you, Lord, for you answered me: and have become my salvation.
4 The stone that the builders rejected: has become the corner-stone.
5 This is the work of the Lord: it is marvellous in our eyes.
6 This is the day that the Lord has made: let us rejoice and be glad in it.
7 Blessed is he who comes in the name of the Lord: from the house of the Lord we bless you.
8 The Lord is God and he has given us light: with branches in your hands join the procession and march round the altar.
9 You are my God, and I will praise you: I will proclaim your greatness.
10 Give thanks to the Lord for he is good: and his mercy endures for ever.

from Psalm 118

1 We put away all malice and guile: all hypocrisy, jealousy and slander.
2 Like new-born babes we thirst for pure spiritual milk: for we have tasted the kindness of the Lord.
3 We come to Christ our Lord: rejected by men, yet chosen by God.
4 Like living stones we are built into a spiritual temple: we are a holy priesthood, offering spiritual sacrifices to God through Jesus Christ.
5 We are a chosen race, a royal priesthood, a holy nation: God's own people, chosen to proclaim his wonderful acts.
6 Let our conduct reflect the good deeds of God: that all may praise him on the day of his coming.

from 1 Peter 2

1 Come, let us praise the Lord: shout for joy to the rock of our
   salvation.
2 Let us come into his presence with thanksgiving: and rejoice with
   songs of praise.
3 For the Lord is a great God: and a great king above all gods.
4 In his hands are the depths of the earth: the heights of the
   mountains are his.
5 The sea is his, he made it: his hands formed the dry land.
6 Come, let us worship and bow down: and kneel before the Lord
   our maker.
7 For he is our God: and we are his people, and the sheep of his
   pasture.

from Psalm 95

1 God has made known his secret: he has revealed it by his Spirit in
   his apostles and prophets.
2 The Gentiles are fellow-heirs with the Jews, members of the same
   body: partakers of a promise made in Christ Jesus.
3 God, creator of all things, kept his mystery hidden through all past
   ages: but now the wisdom of God is made manifest.
4 He did this according to his eternal purpose: which he has realized
   in Christ Jesus our Lord.
5 In union with Christ we may go into God's presence: with the
   confidence born of trust in him.
6 We fall on our knees before God the Father: from whom every
   family in heaven and on earth is named.
7 May God, from the riches of his glory, make us strong in his
   Spirit: and Christ make his home in our hearts.
8 May we be rooted and grounded in love: that we may understand
   how broad and long, how high and deep, is Christ's love.
9 May we know the love of Christ which surpasses knowledge: that
   we may be filled with the very nature of God.

from Ephesians 3

1 Bless the Lord, O my soul: O Lord my God, how great you are.
2 The clouds are your chariots: and you ride on the wings of the wind.
3 The winds are your messengers: and the flames of lightning are your servants.
4 You have set the earth on its foundations: and it shall never be moved.
5 You make the springs flow in the valley: and the rivers run between the hills.
6 They give water to every wild animal: and in the trees nearby the birds nest and sing.
7 From the sky you send rain on the hills: and the earth is filled with the fruits of your work.
8 You cause the grass to grow for the cattle: and the plants to grow for man.
9 The earth is full of your creatures: and the oceans teem with living things.
10 All depend on you: you give them food according to their needs.
11 May the glory of the Lord last for ever: may the Lord rejoice in his creation.

from Psalm 104

1 I am the true vine: and my Father is the vine-dresser.
2 Every branch that bears fruit he prunes: that it may bear more fruit.
3 You are made clean by my word: abide in me, and I will abide in you.
4 A branch cannot bear fruit by itself but must remain in the vine: so you cannot bear fruit unless you remain in me.
5 I am the vine: and you are the branches.
6 If you abide in me and my words abide in you: ask whatever you wish, and it shall be done for you.
7 By this shall my Father be glorified: you shall bear much fruit.

from John 15

1 As new branches sprout from a stump: so a new king will arise from among the descendants of David.

2 The spirit of the Lord shall rest upon him: the spirit of wisdom and insight, of counsel and power.

3 The spirit of knowledge and the fear of the Lord shall come to him: he shall delight in obeying the Lord.

4 He shall not judge by what his eyes see: or decide by what his ears hear.

5 But he shall judge the poor with justice: and defend the rights of the helpless.

6 Integrity shall be the loincloth round his waist: faithfulness the belt round his hips.

7 The wolf shall live with the lamb: the leopard lie down with the kid.

8 The calf and the lion shall feed together: and little children take care of them.

9 The earth shall be full of the knowledge of the Lord: as the waters cover the sea.

from Isaiah 11

1 God has revealed to us his secret wisdom through the Spirit: the Spirit searches everything, even the depths of God.

2 It is only a person's own spirit that knows his thoughts: so also only God's Spirit knows the thoughts of God.

3 We have not received the spirit of the world: but the Spirit sent by God, that we may understand his gifts.

4 The man without the Spirit cannot receive his gifts: he cannot understand them nor judge their value.

5 We who have the Spirit can judge the value of all things: and are judged by no one.

6 We speak in words taught by the Spirit: in the Spirit we have the mind of Christ.

from 1 Corinthians 2

1 I will bring my people out of the nations: and gather them together.
2 I will unite them: and they shall no longer be divided.
3 I will purify them: and they shall be free from the ways in which they sin and betray me.
4 I will give them one king, one shepherd: and they shall faithfully obey my laws.
5 I will make a covenant of peace with them: and they shall live for ever in my land.
6 I will bless them: and they shall multiply.
7 I will dwell with them and be their God: and they shall be my people.

from Ezekiel 37

1 There shall be a new heaven and a new earth: the first heaven and the first earth shall pass away.
2 Behold, I make my home with mankind: they shall be my people, and I will be their God.
3 I will wipe away every tear from their eyes, for death shall be no more: I will make all things new.
4 I am the Alpha and the Omega: the beginning and the end.
5 Whoever wins the victory, I will be his God: and he shall be my son.

from Revelation 21

62 A NEW COMMANDMENT

1 Lord, how I love your law: it is my meditation all the day.
2 I am wiser than all my teachers: for I study your commandments.
3 I am wiser than the old men: for I obey your precepts.
4 How sweet are your words to my tongue: sweeter than honey to my mouth.
5 Your word is a lamp to guide me: a light to my path.
6 Your word will last for ever: it is eternal in the heavens.
7 Your faithfulness endures from one generation to another: as firm as the earth which you created.
8 I love your law: your word is my hope.

from Psalm 119

1 I give you a new commandment: love one another.
2 As I love you: so you are to love one another.
3 As I give my life for you: so you are to give your life for your brothers.
4 Love is not merely words and talk: true love shows itself in action.
5 If you have love one for another: all men will know that you are my disciples.
6 Live in the truth as the Father commands you: love one another in obedience to the commandments of God.

from John 13, 1 John 3 and 2 John

1 I am in trouble: like a hungry man who finds no fruit on the trees, nor grapes on the vines.
2 There is not one honest man left on the earth: there is no one who is loyal to God.
3 Put no confidence in your neighbour nor trust your friend: guard what you say even to your wife.
4 Sons treat their fathers with contempt, and daughters rise up against their mothers: a man's enemies are within his house.
5 But I will look to the Lord: I will wait for the God of my salvation.
6 We are in darkness, but the Lord will be our light: we have fallen, but we shall rise again.
7 There is no God like you, O Lord: you are faithful and confident in your love.

from Micah 7

1 I came to cast fire upon the earth: how I wish it were already kindled.
2 Do not think I have come to bring peace on earth: not peace, but a sword.
3 Nation will rise against nation: kingdom against kingdom.
4 In one house they will be divided: parents against children, children against parents, brother against brother.
5 Everyone will hate you because of me: but he who endures to the end will be saved.
6 For my sake you will be brought to trial before rulers and kings: this will be your opportunity to bear witness.
7 Do not be afraid: do not fear those who kill the body but cannot kill the soul.
8 Whatever is covered up will be revealed: and every secret will be made known.
9 What I am telling you in the dark you must repeat in the light: what you have heard in private you must proclaim from the housetops.
10 The gospel of the kingdom will be preached throughout the world: and then the end will come.

from Matthew 10 and 24, and Luke 12 and 21

64 THE THRONE OF GRACE

1 O Lord, our Lord: how great is your name throughout the earth.
2 Your praise reaches up to the heavens: it is sung by children and babies.
3 I look up to the heavens, the work of your fingers: the moon and the stars which you set in place.
4 What is man that you should think of him: or the son of man that you should care for him?
5 Yet you have made him little less than a god: you have crowned him with glory and splendour.
6 You have made him lord over your creation: he is the ruler of all things.
7 All sheep and oxen, all the beasts of the field: the birds of the air and the fish of the sea.
8 Lord, our Lord: how great is your name throughout the earth.

from Psalm 8

1 We have a great high priest who has passed through the heavens: Jesus, the Son of God.
2 He can sympathize with all our weaknesses: for he has been tempted in every way that we are, yet without sinning.
3 In his days on earth Jesus offered up prayers and supplications: with tears he cried to God to save him from death.
4 He learned obedience through his sufferings: and, being made perfect, he became the source of eternal life for all who obey him.
5 He can save those who draw near to God through him: he lives to intercede with God for them.
6 He is holy, blameless and unstained: he is exalted above the heavens.
7 So let us with confidence draw near the throne of grace: that we may receive mercy and find grace in time of need.

from Hebrews 4, 5 and 7

65 THE VICTORY OF THE CROSS

1 My devoted servant bears the sins of many: for his sake I forgive them.
2 It was my will that he should suffer: he offered his life in atonement.
3 He surrendered himself to death: he shared the fate of sinful men.
4 He suffered the punishment of sinners: and he prayed that they might be forgiven.
5 So he will see his heirs: I shall prolong his life, that through him my will may be done.
6 He will see the fruit of his anguish: and he will be satisfied.

from Isaiah 53

1 Christ Jesus had the nature of God: but he did not try to remain equal with God.
2 Instead he freely emptied himself, taking the form of a servant: and was born in the likeness of men.
3 He humbled himself and walked the path of obedience all the way to death: his death on the cross.
4 Therefore God has raised him to the highest place: and given him the name which is above every name.
5 That at the name of Jesus every knee shall bow: in heaven and on earth and in the world below.
6 And every tongue shall proclaim that Jesus Christ is Lord: to the glory of God the Father.

from Philippians 2

1 The Lord will appear above his people: his arrows will flash out like lightning.

2 The Sovereign Lord will sound the trumpet: and march forth in the whirlwind from the south.

3 The Lord Almighty will protect his people: and he will set them free.

4 He will have compassion on them: and lead them back home.

5 He will save his people: as a shepherd saves his flock from danger.

6 They will shine in his land: like the jewels of a crown.

7 The grain will make the young men flourish: and new wine the maidens.

8 How good and beautiful the land will be: they will be glad for what the Lord has done.

from Zechariah 9 and 10

1 Holy Father, protect my disciples in the power of your name: the name you gave me.

2 While I was with them I kept them safe: I guarded them by the power of your name.

3 I have given them your word: and the world hates them, because they do not belong to the world.

4 I do not ask you to take them out of the world: but to keep them from evil.

5 Sanctify them in the truth: your word is truth.

6 As you sent me into the world, so I have sent them: for their sake I consecrate myself, that they may be consecrated in truth.

from John 17

1   You have turned justice into wormwood: and cast integrity to the ground.
2   You hate the man who challenges injustice: who speaks the truth.
3   You oppress the poor and needy and rob their grain: you persecute the righteous and turn aside the needy.
4   I despise your religious festivals: I take no delight in your solemn assemblies.
5   Take away from me the noise of your songs: I will not listen to the melody of your harps.
6   Instead let justice flow like a stream: and righteousness like a river that never runs dry.
7   Seek good and not evil that you may live: the Lord, the God of Hosts, will be with you.
8   Seek justice for all: and I shall be merciful.
9   The day is coming when I shall plant my people on the land I gave them: they will never again be pulled up.
10   The corn will grow faster than it can be harvested: the grape faster than the wine can be made.
11   The mountains will drip with sweet wine: and the hills will flow with it.
12   I will bring my people back to their land: the Lord your God has spoken.

from Amos 5 and 9

1   Come, you that are blessed by my Father: inherit the kingdom prepared for you from the foundation of the world.
2   I was hungry and you fed me: I was thirsty and you gave me drink.
3   I was a stranger and you welcomed me: I was naked and you clothed me.
4   I was sick and you visited me: I was in prison and you came to me.
5   When you did these things for the least of my brothers: you did them for me.

from Matthew 25

1 Break the chains of wickedness and the yoke of injustice: let the oppressed go free.
2 Share your bread with the hungry and open your homes to the poor: give clothes to the naked.
3 Then my favour will shine on you like the morning sun: and your wounds shall be quickly healed.
4 I will always be present with you: when you pray I will answer you.
5 Put an end to oppression, to every gesture of contempt, to every evil word: then I will make you strong and well.
6 Give food to the hungry, care for those in need: then I will guide you and fill you with good things.
7 You will be like a watered garden: like a spring that never runs dry.
8 You will find joy in serving me: you will be honoured throughout the world.

from Isaiah 58

1 Blessed are the poor in spirit: for theirs is the kingdom of heaven.
2 Blessed are those who mourn: for they shall be comforted.
3 Blessed are the meek: for they shall inherit the earth.
4 Blessed are those who hunger and thirst for righteousness: for they shall be satisfied.
5 Blessed are the merciful: for they shall obtain mercy.
6 Blessed are the pure in heart: for they shall see God.
7 Blessed are the peacemakers: for they shall be called the children of God.
8 Blessed are those who are persecuted for righteousness' sake: for theirs is the kingdom of heaven.

from Matthew 5

1 The Lord is my shepherd: I shall want for nothing.
2 He will let me rest in pastures of young grass: and lead me beside still waters.
3 He will refresh my soul: and guide me in the paths of righteousness for his name's sake.
4 When I walk through the valley of the darkness of death I shall fear no evil: for you are with me, your crook and staff will be my comfort.
5 You spread a banquet before me in front of my enemies: you anoint my head with oil and my cup overflows.
6 I know that your goodness and mercy will be with me all the days of my life: and I shall dwell in the house of the Lord for ever.

from Psalm 23

1 When the last trumpet sounds we shall all be changed: in the twinkling of an eye.
2 When the trumpet sounds we shall all be changed: the dead will be raised immortal.
3 This perishable nature must put on the imperishable: this mortal nature must put on immortality.
4 The sting of death is sin: the power of sin is the law.
5 But thanks be to God: he gives us victory through our Lord Jesus Christ.
6 Death is swallowed up: victory is complete.
7 O death, where is your victory: O death, where is your sting?

from 1 Corinthians 15

1 My heart rejoices in the Lord: for he has saved me.

2 No one is holy like the Lord: there is no rock like our God.

3 Stop your load boasting: silence your proud words.

4 For the Lord is a God of knowledge: he governs all that men do.

5 The bows of the mighty are broken: but the weak grow strong.

6 Those who are well fed now hire themselves out for bread: but the hungry hunger no more.

7 The Lord raises the poor from the dust: he lifts the needy from the ash-heap.

8 He protects the faithful, but the wicked disappear in darkness: for a man cannot triumph in his own strength.

9 He will give power to his king: he will make the chosen one victorious.

from 1 Samuel 2

1 My soul proclaims the greatness of the Lord: my spirit rejoices in God my saviour.

2 For he has remembered his lowly servant: from this day all generations will call me blessed.

3 The Almighty has done great things for me: and holy is his name.

4 He shows mercy to those who honour him: from generation to generation.

5 He has stretched out his mighty arm: and has scattered the proud in their conceit.

6 He has cast down the mighty from their thrones: and lifted up the lowly.

7 He has filled the hungry with good things: and sent the rich away empty.

8 He has come to the help of his servant Israel: remembering his promise of mercy.

9 The promise he made to our fathers: to Abraham and his children for ever.

from Luke 1

71 TESTING AND REJOICING

1 I will send my messenger to prepare a way for me: to proclaim my covenant.
2 I will suddenly enter my temple: but will you be able to endure the day of my coming?
3 I will be like strong soap: like the fire that refines metal.
4 My messenger will purify my people and refine them like gold and silver: till they are fit to be offered to me.
5 I will draw near to you in judgement: but you need have no fear.
6 I am the Lord and I will not change: you shall not be consumed.
7 Turn back to me: and I will turn to you.

from Malachi 3

1 Blessed be the God and Father of our Lord Jesus Christ: grace and peace are ours in full measure.
2 By his great mercy he gave us new birth by raising Jesus Christ from death: he has filled us with a living hope.
3 Now we suffer under trials of many kinds: soon we shall receive an inheritance that nothing can destroy.
4 Now we are tested like gold in fire, that our faith may endure: soon we shall receive praise and glory when Christ is revealed.
5 We love him though we do not see him: we believe in him though we do not know him.
6 We rejoice with joy beyond words: for we are receiving his salvation, the goal of our faith.
7 We must be stripped, ready for action, perfectly self-controlled: we should fix our hope on the grace of Christ.
8 We must be obedient to God: we should be holy, as God who called us is holy.
9 We have been born anew: through the living and abiding word of God.

from 1 Peter 1

72 THE SPIRIT OF FREEDOM

1 Give thanks to the Lord for his goodness: for his love is eternal.

2 Let these be the words of the Lord's redeemed: the people he has rescued from the oppressors' power.

3 Some went astray in the wilderness: they found no path to a city.

4 Then they cried to the Lord in their trouble: he saved them from their distress.

5 He led them by the right paths: to a city where they could live.

6 Some sat in darkness and in deathly shadow: prisoners suffering in chains.

7 Then they cried to the Lord in their trouble: he saved them from their distress.

8 He brought them out of darkness and gloom: he broke their chains in pieces.

9 Some were sick from their sinful ways: they had come to the gates of death.

10 Then they cried to the Lord in their trouble: he saved them from their distress.

11 He sent his word and healed them: and saved them from the grave.

12 Let them thank God for his goodness: for his wonderful works to the children of men.

from Psalm 107

1 Christ has set us free: we have been called to freedom.

2 Do not submit again to the yoke of slavery: do not use your freedom as a licence for sin.

3 Let the Spirit direct your lives: for the Spirit has given us life.

4 Sinful nature produces anger and envy: it causes enmity and strife, it divides people into parties and factions.

5 The fruits of the Spirit are love and patience: it produces peace and kindness, gentleness and self-control.

6 We who belong to Christ have crucified our sinful nature: the Spirit will bring us to eternal life.

from Galatians 5 and 6